"Dogs are often said to be man's best friend. While they are fun, loyal and bring joy to us in many ways, the distinguishing characteristic of our dogs is their complete, total unconditional love. For anyone of faith, we would have to dispute the claim and surely say God is man's best friend, and again because of the unconditional love He has for us. I appreciate Tom writing this book and sharing his love of his dog and the inspiration it has brought him."
—Randy Boyd, founder, CEO and chairman of PetSafe (A Division of Radio Systems), Commissioner of Economic Development for Tennessee

"As a true dog lover, this book really touched my heart. Tom has written a great story about his relationship with his dog, Mango, that made me more aware of why dogs do the funny and sometimes silly things that often amuse and sometimes confuse their adult companions. It's also a powerful journey in faith that proves you really can put worry aside when we place our trust in God. This is a great example of how God teaches us to love unconditionally."
—Louise Mandrell, country music legend and dog lover

"When Job was sorely tested by life and the people were taunting him for his misfortunes, he defended himself by saying, '...ask the animals and they will teach you' (Job 12:7). Author Tom Baker does just that in his new book, *One Dog's Faith*: 'How my dog helped me learn to trust God and overcome chronic worrying.' At a low point in his career and desperate for guidance, Baker turns to the family's four-year-old Spaniel mix for answers. By thinking deeply about what God intended to teach us through our dogs, Baker found more answers than most folks could dig up in all the self-help books in a bookstore. What he finds is proof of the truism that the answers we seek are all around us if only we look hard enough. *One Dog's Faith* is a loving meditation of 'dogness' that will resonate with dog lovers and show them the family pooch in a totally new light."
—Craig Miller, VP of Original Programming, INSP Network

"Dog lovers of almost any age will love this! What a fun way to talk about faith and trust in our amazing God."
—Bishop Mary Virginia Taylor, Holston Conference of the United Methodist Church

"Dogs are great rescuers. They bark when they see smoke filling the room of their sleeping masters. Climbing the rubble and carnage of the fallen Twin Towers on 911, their noses detected victims and brought them to safety. I've watched in amazement as a dog navigated a bustling New York City intersection and escorted his blind master safely to the other side! Tom Baker's humorous, warm and whimsical book, *One Dog's Faith*, shows us another incredible feat that our hairy canine friends can do—help someone connect with the love, grace and peace of God."
—Tony Nolan, minister, mentor, author, touring pastor for WinterJam

"It's been said a friend doubles your joys and halves your sorrows. That's true. Our dogs are our friends. Tom's book provides remarkable insights into the power of his friendship with his dog. Mango is not only his friend, Mango emerges as a teacher and healer...an instrument in the hand of God. Tom's story is one that needs to be read and shared. It is an awakening. God can use our friends (our pets) to help us and he does. Thank you for writing this book."
—Hallerin Hilton Hill, radio/TV host, teacher, trainer, author

"*One Dog's Faith* is written by a man of faith. It has been my pleasure to know Tom and his family for many years, and this book has definitely been inspired! There are great messages and examples that apply to everyone. The fact is, you don't need to read this book, you *deserve* to. You will be encouraged, inspired, and delighted as you read about Mango and her faith."
—Dave Gorden, motivational speaker and former president, National Speakers Association

"I have known Tom for over 25 years, first as his friend and colleague, and now as his pastor. I have marveled at the depths of his creativity and the integrity of his faith. That same faith and creativity have intersected in his new book to reveal a fascinating faith journey. Don't miss the blessings that are right before you, wagging its tail."

—Rev. Larry Trotter, Senior Pastor, Concord United Methodist

"I really think you are on to something here! This book is a great way to get the 'good news' out there! There are a lot of dog lovers who will be very intrigued by this book, some of whom may hear for the first time, or hear again after a long time, the good news of our Lord."

—Rev. Nathan Malone, United Methodist district superintendent

"Having had the privilege of being Mango's veterinarian since she became a member of the Baker family, I definitely believe that she is a special soul. Having said that, I believe that all animals are special and that God has unique missions for each of them. Working with animals daily for the last twenty-two years, I have seen firsthand the remarkable connection and bond that develop between our animal companions and their families. I don't believe that it is coincidental that they seem to work diligently to mirror God's amazing qualities, or that dog is God spelled backwards!"

—Dr. Cristi Moser, DVM, Bluegrass Animal Hospital

"You'll never look at the family dog the same way again. All dog lovers know that there's something sweet and special about the canine members of their family, but now we understand so much more through the eyes of Mango. Why do dogs stick their heads out the car window? Why do they sniff one another's rears? How do they somehow know what their family needs, and they're right there to give it? *One Dog's Faith* will make you laugh, it will make you cry, and it will make you run and hug your dog."

—Mark and Frances Smith, Authors, *Cleft of the Rock*,
Cleftoftherock.org

"Maybe it's no coincidence that the word God spelled backwards is dog. Dogs are loyal, trusting and forgiving, not unlike our maker. Dogs bring such joy into our lives and so does God if we let Him. I have known Tom Baker and his family for many years. Tom is a devoted husband, father, pet owner and above all else a deeply devoted Christian. His faith is constant and pure and never wavering. In his book, *One Dog's Faith*, Tom and his dog, Mango, teach us to keep the faith through good times and bad, to trust the Lord to guide us through life's darkest moments."
—**Thyra Walker, DVM, Forest Park Clinic for Cats and Dogs**

"Love makes us see things, as does fear. Sometimes those things are there and sometimes they aren't. Love and fear also blind, preventing us from seeing the full picture. *One Dog's Faith* shares the vision of a very special dog, Mango. You'll see what she sees. You'll also see more than she sees…and less. Why? Mango loves and fears, just as we do. She sees what's there; she also sees things not there. Often she sees only in part. Her vision gets as muddled by love and fear as ours. God and His love are different. He sees clearly and loves dearly. *One Dog's Faith* provides an extended glimpse of the peace and joy owned by those who trust in God and His love despite our inability to yet see completely."
—**David Horsewood, owner & principal speaker/trainer with Fire by Light LLC, author of *Fire by Light: Real & Relevant Applications***

One Dog's Faith

Tom Baker

E ergreen
PRESS

Mobile, Alabama

ISBN 978-1-58169-633-2
For Worldwide Distribution
Printed in the U.S.A.

Evergreen Press
P.O. Box 191540 • Mobile, AL 36619
800-367-8203

Contents

Acknowledgments

To our Almighty Creator, through your Son, Christ Jesus, my amazing King...you allowed me to witness your life-changing power and grace and enabled me to attain truly powerful peace and hope. Only through you could this have happened. Your ways are perfect and your timing is unmistakable. You have led me through journeys that I would never have chosen but would now never trade. You gave me freedom from destructive worry and instead pointed me to a beautiful, glorious, and exciting outlook. When I had no hope, you said simply, "Open your eyes." I truly thought my life was falling apart when all the while you have been piecing it together. I pray that this book only glorifies you. I am unworthy of the privilege to do this ministry.

To my God-given wife, Michelle. You make every day wonderful. Your unconditional love humbles me. You kept me centered, you pointed me up when I only looked down, you believed in me when I had no belief in myself. You encouraged me when I needed it and grounded me when I thought it was all about me. This would not have happened without your unshakeable faith, encouragement, passion, patience, guidance, and most of all, your love. I totally love you and am excited to experience life (including the challenges) with you.

To my children: Carolyn, Sophie, Chloe, and Cristian. You take my breath away every day. Every victory and every challenge you have makes my life full. I can't believe I am lucky enough to be your dad. God has blessed me with your lives and I can't be more proud.

To my incredible parents, Gene and Dave Baker, who helped me buy in to the love of Christ and dogs from day one and who showed me that compassion, honesty, and love (no matter how many stupid things I might do) are the fabric of life.

To Mango: You really have such a wonderful soul. God put you in our lives for so many reasons. You are doing your God appointed jobs so well. Your unconditional love and true faithfulness were a large part of the inspiration to write this book. It's all in a day's work for you.

Endless thanks also goes to Rev. Larry Trotter, Rev. Wil Cantrel, Rev. Glenna Manning, Rev. Brent Hall, Bishop Mary Virginia Taylor, Rusty Taylor, Dave Gorden, Hallerin Hill, Mark and Fran Smith, David Horsewood, Todd McCoig, Bruce Adams, Stephen Brown and Linda Meyers for your time, advice, patience, godly direction, mentoring, encouragement, and love.

Preface

We all have stories. We all have jobs. We all have things that we were put on this earth to do. Most people think my breed just lies around and sleeps all the time. Well, we do, but we have reasons.

I'm supposed to help people, especially my family. Tom and Michelle are my human adults, and their children are Carolyn, Sophie, Chloe, and Cristian. They all need me, but they have no idea how much.

Let me introduce myself. I'm Mango, female, three years old, sixty pounds . . . a spaniel mix. I'm mixed with about seventy-three other breeds, which makes me unique.

I was a pound dog and had a few homes before this one. My other families couldn't handle my energy. They weren't dog people. Those times were only practice for this home anyway. When I was sent back to the pound, I thought life was over, but God always has great plans during bad times. When things are at their worst, that's when you can see God's work most clearly.

As usual, God's plan worked out perfectly. I had some smaller jobs at those other homes, but those families didn't want help. I tried, but they had no interest in giving me any attention or learning anything from me. They were too preoccupied. It must be how God feels about some people. He tries so hard to help them and love them, but they turn the other way. They miss what God has to offer them. People can sometimes totally miss what a dog has to offer them as well. It's so sad.

And it's true, pound dogs are the best dogs—we have been humbled and completely appreciate a home when we get it. Dogs who are born in homes don't understand. Pound dogs know what abandonment and mistreatment feels like, and when we have it good, we know it.

I'm a little hyperactive. Okay, a lot hyperactive. I love getting into trouble and getting noticed for better or worse. To me, when I get in trouble, I have everyone's attention.

Michelle and Tom came to the Young-Williams Animal Adoption Center to get me. I was competing with something like seventy-five dogs. Tom and Michelle came four or five times and looked at a lot of dogs. I showed them my best, most infectious charm every time they came. They took me out to the play area a few times and we had a blast. All the kids loved me and played with me. I couldn't understand why they didn't just grab me the first time they saw me. I pretty much knew they were going to take me home.

Once they chose me, I tried to act calm, but it didn't exactly turn out that way. I kind of scared them. It's not that I was mean or dangerous. I was just so excited when we got home that I ran, I mean ran all over the house, jumping on tables, chairs, and counters. I ran for thirty minutes while Michelle watched, dumbfounded, with her mouth wide open.

Okay, I totally freaked out, and so did she.

She called Tom and said that this was a mistake and she didn't know what to do. That's when I finally got control of myself. I was so excited to be in my forever home. I couldn't help it. She figured out right then that I had energy and spunk. She figured out that I was nuts; that's just me. Once we got used to each other, though, things became perfect. I was where I was supposed to be.

And now I'm telling you my story . . . our story. When you're finished, I hope you'll understand us dogs better.

Introduction

Dogs are special creatures. They seem to have emotions that are similar to us humans. Their whole being is elevated when we arrive home from even a three-minute trip to the mailbox, and they get truly embarrassed when we put a silly hat on their head or when they're the product of a less-than-perfect haircut. Without a word being spoken, dogs seem to empathize when we feel sick or depressed and need a warm, loving being to lie down beside us. There was no accident or exaggeration when the phrase "man's best friend" was coined. We connect and develop a tremendously deep bond with our dogs. They usually become part of the family they join, and when they're no longer with us, we feel a sadness and sense of loss that is as difficult or sometimes more difficult than losing a human friend or family member.

But is there more? Do dogs have something more than a sweet heart and loving disposition? Is it possible they have a special connection with the Creator? When they look up at the ceiling with complete amazement, are they seeing an angel? Do dogs have jobs they were divinely appointed to do? Do they have a real reason for existence far deeper than eating, playing, and sleeping? Were they put here on earth specifically to help us humans see that God is alive, that God is here with us, and that unconditional love is not only possible but is the only way God works?

There is no evidence to support or refute any of these possibilities. Until we can speak fluent "dog," we're left with only clues into the minds of dogs. So join me in wondering, "What if . . ."

—*Tom Baker*

The ultimate measure of a man is

not where he stands in moments

of comfort and convenience

but where he stands

in times of challenge

and controversy.

– Martin Luther King

*(Maybe it's possible that his dog
came up with this saying first...)*

Above: "Focused, alert, and laying in the garden where I shouldn't be."
Below: "My window to the world!"

Above: "Let's build a snow dog!"
Below: "I love being clean but hate the process." (With Michelle & Cristian)

Above: "Comfortable in my own fur..."
Below: "I love my job!"

Above: "My throne."
Below: "Unconditional love..."

1

What Is My Life?

"The average dog is a nicer person than the average person."

— Andy Rooney (contributor, *60 Minutes*)

"I think dogs are the most amazing creatures; they give unconditional love. For me, they are the role model for being alive."

— Gilda Radner (comedienne)

"Outside of a dog, a book is man's best friend. Inside of a dog, it's too dark to read."

— Groucho Marx (comedian)

"Dogs are better than humans because they know but do not tell." *— Emily Dickinson* (poet)

Tonight it's quiet and peaceful. Everyone else in the house is asleep, but I'm wide awake. I'm on alert when everyone else is slumbering. I have a lot of responsibility and I'm on task. I'll have time to sleep when things are calmer during the day.

I love my home. I spend my nights in the room with Tom and Michelle. They keep their bedroom door closed and I can't ever open it. I lie down against the door and they can't open the door unless they move me . . . which, of course, is the point. Not sure what kind of statement that makes, but it makes a statement. The floor is slippery, so they end up sliding me across the hardwood floor to pull the door open. I like that . . . it's kind of fun. It keeps me in the loop, so to speak. Once they close the door again, I move right back. It's a good challenge . . . for them.

I work hard to always be in the way. I stay in the middle of everything and always know what's going on. Plus, I get more face time. At night, I lie awake, listening for any odd or, more importantly, dangerous sounds. My whole family is asleep so they surely aren't listening. I'm all there is between the danger outside and them.

It's total alert mode for me, which is the normal mode of operation for most any dog. I let everyone know if something doesn't sound, smell, or feel right. It's my job to protect and warn. I can hear ten times more clearly compared to what they hear. I know danger and I know when I need to alert everybody. Tom and Michelle often say, "Be quiet, Mango!" But they don't hear what I hear; it's for them that I sound the alert. I stay awake for most of the night while they sleep, and then they wonder why I sleep so much during the day. It's okay . . . I don't mind. They don't quite understand dogs anyway. Most people don't.

I really do hear something now my ears are up. Is it worth alerting everybody? It's kind of a dull, creepy sound—like a car door that needs grease, slowly opening. It could be a bad guy, a really bad guy. To me, they're all bad guys wanting to get in, and I'm the only thing that can stop them from hurting my family. Shhh, there it is again. Oh wait. Uuuuhhh, it was Tom. They had beans last night. Never mind.

The alarm clock radio goes off. It scares the dickens out of me every time. And they're off! The race begins to see which child makes it to school on time.

I run to help wake up the kids, one of the great perks of my job. Jumping on the bed and giving a good, wet lick in a child's face works much better than what Michelle does, which is to scratch their backs and say, "Good morning, good morn-ing!" She sings that song from *Singin' in the Rain*. Yes, I know that movie. They don't think I watch TV and understand, but I do. It's fuzzy and strange looking, but I enjoy the sounds. I don't see how they enjoy watching it so much, but they do.

They play it too loud to hear a sound from outside . . . which makes it difficult to be on alert. And when dogs bark on TV, it fools me about every fifth time. They all laugh at me when I jump up out of a cold sleep and run to the door, barking at a sound that came from the TV. I stay at the door and bark as if something were really there to make them think I'm working instead of being fooled.

Anyway, the kids are awake but not getting out of bed . . . it's *time* . . . wet, drooling dog tongue all over the face. I don't stop until there's movement. Nothing wakes a kid like warm dog slobber. My job has just begun.

Second things second . . . it's time for a trip into the back-yard to check my "P-Mail" and to scout and make sure everything is as it was last night. Wait, hold on . . . a rabbit has been here. This is not right. Oh, let me at it. I run from one end of the fence to the other. Nothing is supposed to be in this yard that isn't previously approved. And here's rabbit poop . . . even worse. This is *my* yard, where I poop and no one else can poop.

I hear Millie in the background in the neighbor's yard. She's a mountain cur mix. They're nervous and reactive, and they bark at the least little sound. She had a tough night with her humans . . . they have teenagers who stay up most of the night and never get any sleep. I can tell that from her bark, and I can kind of read her thoughts. She had to work overtime keeping everything in line last night.

I don't have time to deal with that right now. Back to important things. I check all corners. The rabbit seems to be MIA now. I can follow its path . . . I know where it has been. I have smelled it before. If I catch that thing, it's bunny and rice. Better yet, bunny in one bite. Who knows exactly what a rabbit might do to my humans?

Worse yet . . . they might take it in as a pet, which of course would take their eyes off of me—and that won't be tolerated. If I squat on the spots where he has been, maybe he won't feel welcome or want to come back . . . and yes, I know it's a he. I can almost smell what color he is. He's not welcome and I should stay out here and find him, but I better go in and help.

Everything else seems clear and I want back in the house. All I have to do is stand by the door and they let me in. They check my feet and wipe them with a towel. I don't especially like that, but I put up with it.

It's my responsibility to entertain, to protect, and sometimes to turn things upside down. This morning, like nearly every morning, I consider it my job to steal a sock and run right when Tom is ready to put it on. It makes life quite interesting. He glances up, giving me *the look*. Breaking point—maybe even a game of tug-of-war might start. What a letdown; he grabs another pair and goes on downstairs.

Maybe the sock has enough drool on it to make my mark so I can find it later.

Okay, maybe he'll play with my favorite rope toy. I can soften it up a little by chewing, and then he'll grab it and throw it. I'll chase it down and bring it back. It's good exercise . . . for him. He needs it. He doesn't ever exercise and he would feel so much better if he did. I need it too. Then I wouldn't go wacko in the house so much. The only exercise he gets is when I steal stuff from him and he chases me. "No" again. I was only able to rub slobber on his leg with the toy and then there it lies, on the ground.

I have got to work harder with him today. He seems stressed. His business is doing pretty badly and he's worried. That's a big responsibility I have—to distract him from stress. Either by playing, loving, or distracting by destruction or better yet by theft, I'll get him out of this.

Chloe, their twelve-year-old daughter, is coming down-stairs now. Good, she's in a hurry . . . that means she always drops part of the lunch that she's making for school. Waiting . . . waiting . . . patience . . . yesssss. A piece of gluten-free toast . . . delicious. My family is all vegan, gluten free, and sugar free. Makes my life a little strange, but they feed me meat. Most families feed their dog out of some bag and the rest of them eat the meat.

Just the opposite here. I eat meat; they don't. Fine with me! They know that I'm made to eat meat . . . I mean, I have sharp canine teeth, made to chew meat. Meat wasn't meant for humans. It was meant for animals on the hunt. My family eats vegetables, beans, nuts, and fruits, which is what their bodies want most. I get meat . . . raw meat and carrot shavings and such, exactly what I need. I'm a lucky dog.

Chloe will be more careful now . . . no more dropped food, at least for a few minutes. Ever since they went vegan, it's been a challenge. Spinach tastes like something a hedgehog ate and pooped off a cliff. But carrots . . . I can get into those. She peels them and I always get a piece of the peel.

Hold on, I hear something . . . something that deserves a major bark. "Get away from my house! You don't want to deal with me!" I bark loud enough for whoever was out there to hear from inside my home. "Be quiet" is the only response I get from my humans.

Chloe is grabbing the almond butter . . . almond butter . . . it's an acquired taste, but since I'm fed only once a day, I'll chomp it in one bite. But apples and pears . . . they put them into their smoothies pretty much every day. I always get a few pieces that Tom cuts off, you know, the parts that humans don't usually eat where the seeds are and around the stem. They could eat those parts, no problem, but they don't like the looks of them so they give them to me. I'm perfectly happy with that. Actually, I'm great with that. Chloe always leaves her crumbs on the counter. Michelle and Tom get on to her about that, but I love it!

When they walk out of the room, the counter is on limits. I can reach to about halfway back, and that's where most of the food crumbs are anyway. If I get caught, it's bad news. It drives Tom crazy. He sends me out of the room and upstairs to the bedroom and shuts the door. Sometimes I get a scolding, but it's still worth it.

I have to be really careful. Food is where I lose my manners, my exemplary behavior. I forget the rules when it comes to food. Actually, I throw the rules out the window for the thought of food. My stomach has a larger brain than my head. Today, it's not gonna happen anyway . . . everybody is in too much of a hurry; the room won't be empty until later, and someone will clean the counter before that.

Sophie bounces downstairs next. She's a little older, fourteen, and always sneaks a snack to me. Just one big-eyed puppy-dog look and she's sunk. I get two chips and a pinch of bread from her sandwich. Tasty.

Now, it's back to trying to irritate Tom . . . he's standing in the kitchen making smoothies. If I lie down right at his feet, right where he's working, he'll step over me five times and then it's trouble time. "Move out of the way, you crazy dog!" He's stressed . . . nothing that a wet, slobbery rope won't change. I'll rub it up against his leg and get a major rise out of him. He'll feel it, reach down to his leg, and get slimed. It works nearly every time, but today still nothing.

Things are tense today . . . the family is running late. Tom is putting a dark cloud over everybody, even worse than usual. When he's not stressed it's much better, but it's tough today. It's the morning battle zone, kind of. I can be a peacekeeper if they acknowledge me. Tom has got to lighten up. Worrying will get him nowhere but further down in the dumps. It doesn't change anything, and he'll regret being this down when things work out like God planned. Michelle keeps telling him to let it all go.

Sophie is upset because she can't find that one pink shirt that she wanted to wear. She had it in her mind last night that this pink shirt was the *only* shirt that would work. I helped her . . . okay, I stood with her when she picked it. Nothing else will do . . . glad I'm not a fourteen-year-old girl in high school. That's pressure. I may have drama in me . . .

usually to get my back rubbed . . . but nothing like a fourteen-year-old.

She gives in to my leaning against her and stops for a scratch behind the ear. I try to get her to scratch right above my tail . . . I can't ever reach that and it itches all the time. When someone scratches it, it just itches more.

Sophie has a test today. She stayed up late studying and is going to study more this morning while she's getting ready. You know, I could pass the test with flying colors. All I have to do is eat the notes she has, go outside and wait a few minutes, then let those papers pass right through . . . the natural way. I ate some crayons off the floor last night, so today's passing will be quite colorful—flying colors, get it? I'm proud of my creative designs in the yard.

Chloe is upset because she can't find a school paper that's due today. She seems to misplace things a lot. The creative type never puts stuff back. She's like their oldest daughter, Carolyn, age twenty-four—the arteeeeest. She lives in an apartment not far from here. I've been there. Why do they call them apartments when they're so close together? Just a question.

Come to think of it, I don't put stuff back either, but they always pick up after me. I believe that I'm a creative type too. I make messes; I make designs in the yard with pieces of chewed toys and previously eaten crayons. My crayon designs in the yard should be eligible for design awards. It takes real imagination to do that.

We have a cat that lives here too. Her name is Kiwi. Don't ask me why they name animals after food in this house, I am not sure. We don't see her much except while she's lying in a chair or in the sun somewhere. Her job is basically to have a calming effect on our humans. We don't work together much at all. She does her thing; I do mine. Okay, she catches bugs sometimes. Not much glory in that.

Oh, then there's the dishwasher. When someone loads the dishwasher with dirty dishes . . . I consider it not only my job, but a privilege, to be the prewash stand-in. They always seem to complain that the dishwasher doesn't clean the dishes very well, so that's where I come in. They sometimes leave the door open while they load it, and I clean the dishes. I can stick my nose between the plates and bowls to lick them; they don't even need this crazy machine. Good grief, why not just set the plates on the floor and let me clean them? Win-win to me.

Lately I've had a problem with the dishwasher, though. At times I get a little focused on prewashing the dishes and maybe I position myself inside the dishwasher. Like maybe I stand up inside the place where the dishes are with the door fully open. Certainly, I get in trouble for that . . . but there are times when my people leave the room with the dishwasher door open, and I quickly find myself standing inside it . . . and then it happens. I'm hooked, and not in a good way. Somehow, my collar gets hooked on the rack thing that holds the dishes. Not good. There I'm, innocently licking dishes, and C+R+A+S+H! The rack thing full of dishes is following me all over the room. The crashes keep coming and the whole family comes running in. That scares me more and I run harder. What's worse? This thing hooked on while I'm trying to get away making loud crash sounds or them yelling at me to *stop*! At least I know where I've been . . . an ever-growing trail of broken dishes trails behind me.

For some reason they decide to not let me clean dishes anymore. . . I need a hug.

9

Tom's Perspective: Dogs watch everything we do. I hope their memories are not that great. I believe they look at us humans in total amazement, not because they're envious but because they believe we're out of our minds. I can tell that Mango simply wants us to be safe and happy. She looks as if most of the time she's either playing, eating, or sleeping. But a slight bit more observance reveals that she has a purpose in most everything that she does, and she takes that purpose seriously.

2

I Feel the Worry

I was a pound dog, if you remember. There were nights in that place where I had no idea if tomorrow was going to happen. Most dog shelters don't keep all their animals, if you know what I mean. After a while, if a dog doesn't get chosen by someone, that dog is labeled. After a longer while, that label becomes more than a label; it becomes a problem. Shelters can't keep all of their "problems." After a while I noticed that some "problems" weren't around anymore. I figured that out, and reality set in. I had two choices: to worry, or to pray, do my best, and trust God for the perfect outcome. It's funny: when you pray and trust God, the best usually does happen. It may not be what we want, but it will ultimately be what is best for all concerned. It's a choice, sometimes a difficult one, but I chose to pray for my owners to be not only fun people, but good, loving, God-fearing humans. I got my wish.

Chloe and Sophie get in trouble for not cleaning up their stuff. Chloe can't find her school paper, and I didn't steal it. At least, I didn't this time. She's worried. If she doesn't find it, then she'll receive a bad grade. Certainly I'd take claim of the infraction if I had anything to do with it. I have to do something to break up this tension. I rub up against Sophie . . . I lick her hand . . . nothing. I nibble at Chloe's leg, "Ouch, Mango," is all I get. I didn't even bite hard . . . talk about drama. Then they push me away because they think I'm in the way. I'll think of something.

Aha, here's the real plan of action . . . tug-of-war with the five-year-old, Cristian. They just got him up and I can drag him around the kitchen floor. That always raises eyebrows and lightens the mood. This is how the worries of the morning can all but disappear.

I love my job. Cristian is the coolest kid ever. He loves to play and we're *very best* buddies. He is always full of life, and his only purpose, it seems, is to smile and enjoy. That's what life should be about. He dives on me and lies all over me and *I love it*! Tug-of-war is our game, and it's never a letdown with him.

If only the older kids could be kids again. That's what God wants out of everybody . . . to be like a kid. That's the secret. Watch five-year-olds . . . they want everything to just be fun and leave the worrying to the worriers. The worst thing to a five-year-old is not getting to watch a TV show, getting something taken away because they're in trouble, or having to go to bed even if they're completely exhausted.

Michelle has been signing school papers. She stays home when Cristian is in preschool so I usually have more time with her. She keeps everybody going so the morning will end on a positive note. She knows how to redirect and get little squabbles to end nicely.

It's a somewhat tense morning . . . pretty common. Worry, worry, worry. I know what they're thinking: Sophie has a test and she doesn't feel like she knows the material very well, and Chloe has a challenge in gym to do forty-three sit-ups in one minute. She's scared about that because so far, she has only been able to do thirty-eight. Usually when she practices, I have to lick her in the face, and that makes her lose count and have to start all over. That's the way I roll.

And Tom's still worried about his business. It's been in trouble for over two years. He owes a lot of people money. I can't understand why he's so freaky about it. He has employees and he feels responsible for them. How do I know? Dogs can kind of read minds. Well, not like word for word, although sometimes we can. We can read body language, smell different emotions, and sense what's going on inside. And, of course, we hear things as well. Most importantly, we know things . . . especially worry, fear, and trouble. We are not supposed to let humans know that we can. But if they look hard enough, they can see it in our eyes.

We just know things . . . it's a God thing. His Spirit tells us many things. We don't hear Him talking; we just feel it. He lets us know when we're barking up the wrong tree, so to speak. Sometimes we don't listen, but He gives us instructions and tells us what He wants us to do.

Tom's Perspective: What if that's true? Do dogs have more going on inside that fur than just plain, "Feed me, *feed me!*" They seem to have compassion and a true sense of feeling our pain and worry. We'll never quite know on this plane of existence, but we'll find out later. It's nice to feel that Mango does try to keep smiles in our home when things get thick. When there are stern conversations or feelings of fear and worry, Mango always seems to be close by and up to something. I can look at her and see the wheels spinning in her mind. I'll say that I get a sense of peace sometimes when she rubs up against me or jumps on me out of nowhere.

3

What Would They Do Without Me?

It's time for Tom to take the girls to school, which
means he will want to take me out in the backyard for
my business. It's insurance that I won't do anything
inside the house. That makes this the best time for
me to hide behind a door and make him look for me.
There are about ten places that I normally hide, so
Tom has to look in every one of them. I never keep it
the same, and if he finds me too quickly, I'll create a
new one. Right now I'm under the dining room table,
and he's way off . . . somewhere back in a bedroom
yelling for me. More exercise for him. I hear him
calling. Quiet . . . shhh.

My family doesn't know what they would do without
me; I mean, they don't know how they could live without
me. I mean, they have no idea how they could survive without
me. How could they? Their lives would be boring. Their lives
would be empty. Their lives would be unprotected and certainly more frightening without my wisdom, vision, and most
importantly, my companionship.

Unimaginable . . . Mango-less. I see things they don't see. I
sense their fear . . . not only the fear such as being scared . . .
but the fear that things will not turn out okay. I know when

they're afraid of life and when they're uneasy. That's when I can comfort or I can distract. It's a tough choice, but I usually can pick pretty well. Comfort from a dog is a God-designed thing.

Okay, I know what you're thinking . . . yes, God is real. He made everything. He's always there. And He cares about all of us, deeply. He made dogs to help and comfort humans. He made a lot of things just for humans, but we dogs are here as helpers. We know that, and we accept that. We serve. Some people don't realize that dogs are here for a purpose, so some dogs are left out in the cold and are not used for what they were designed to do. It's sad.

Dogs have the amazingly fun but sometimes tough job to lighten everything up. We try to be there in the troubled times for a nudge or lick of love, to lie down next to our humans when they don't want to talk, to tear up a favorite shoe when they need a real distraction, and to be the perfect companion when they're lonely. We have many ways to try and equalize humans.

Cats have the same job, but they do it in a much different way. I don't feel they do much of anything, but they do have real jobs.

Dogs can dig deep into a home and give their humans all kinds of things. No other animal has this kind of responsibility directly from God. We are supposed to add warmth to a home. We add love. We add security and protection. Many homes are so lacking in love. This home where I live now is not lacking in love—they are just distracted. . . mostly from worrying. They have love and they have God in their hearts. That makes our jobs so much easier. They are open to what God can do in their lives. Dogs warn and protect; we distract, we give love, we eat . . . okay, I threw that last one in.

God gives dogs those jobs and we follow orders. I would rather suffer than disobey God. We get our instructions in our minds. The instructions come to us and we understand. Humans say they feel nudges or that "something told me to do that" feeling. It's the same instinct. Humans sometimes don't trust those feelings and don't realize they're coming directly from the one and only God.

The instructions we get from God are real, but instead of blowing them off like most humans, we dogs trust and follow His directions. It's His Holy Spirit talking. You may not realize that the Holy Spirit is there, but He is, in a big way. He talks to your heart all the time . . . if you believe. Dogs will go to great lengths to do our jobs. We will go without food, we'll go through pain, and we're very patient. If I have to wait all day to do my job to help my humans, no problem . . . I'll do it.

We live in a roomy people house in the middle of a big neighborhood. There are human kids everywhere and they ring the doorbell all the time. It drives me completely crazy. I always think it's somebody outside ready to do something bad to us. The door opens . . . and it's a kid. I keep barking. Lets them know I'm here to take care of everybody and not to be messed with. That's what I'm supposed to do. Everybody in this house tries to shush me when I bark . . . but it's for their own good. I let them know when something is different or dangerous. I know it's loud, but it's supposed to be.

New people come to the house and they don't smell like things I'm used to smelling. I tell everybody that these strangers might be dangerous. They tell me to be quiet and everything is okay, but my nose is ten times more powerful than theirs. I can smell when something is not normal. I can smell when humans have bad intentions. And I know when something bad is going to happen. I'll speak my mind and let them know, even if I get in trouble.

Wait, I gotta scratch. Yeah . . . right there, that's it. I have to roll on my back to get this one. Why don't they stop and help me? They could scratch the top of my back better than I can.

One of the best vantage points in the house is the top of the stairs. It overlooks the front door. I hang my head and front feet over the edge of the top step. I can hear everything in the house and get to whoever needs me very fast. I can be halfway down the stairs before I realize I have moved. I am always either positioned where I can watch for danger, or I am laying down close to a human, the one who could need me the most

I love to play, I love to run (especially in the house), and I love to mess with things. Whenever the kids run and play, I run with them . . . although I usually knock somebody over in the process.

I have to hide stuff to see if they can find it. I chew things to smithereens and, of course, wrestle with the big pillow on top of Tom and Michelle's bed. Sometimes I have my reasons, although sometimes I just have to do it. Chewing human things is worth the trouble . . . toys, pencils, underwear (my favorite . . . very interesting tastes in those; they wonder why my breath is bad sometimes), crayons, and whatever I can manage to sneak in the house from the backyard. It's floss, it's mouthwash, and it's exercise. It's getting noticed.

I can always find new things to try and new stuff to tear up. I hide under the dining room table, and nobody finds me until things are chewed nearly unrecognizable. I try to make it to where they can't tell what it was that I pulverized . . . sometimes I don't get in as much trouble that way. Bringing things in from the backyard always gets a rise out of everybody.

Ah yes, the backyard . . . that's my kingdom. I'm an inside dog, but they let me go outside in the backyard pretty much whenever I want. A bell hangs by the door going out on the deck. All I have to do is ring it with my nose and they open the door. The backyard is pretty big and fenced, and I can hear and smell what goes on for miles. Humans can't. How do I know? I hear something plain as day and they don't even tilt their head.

The other dogs in the neighborhood mouth off here and there. They try to tell me that their house is better than mine, their humans are smarter than mine, and their food is better than mine. But I know I have it good. I eat raw meat, I have a big yard, and my humans are quite fun.

The dogs around the hood keep me in the know too. They warn me about what's going on close by, but they also tell me what the Spirit has told them. All the dogs chime in to add our certain piece to the story. We all know when it's going to storm. We all know when the trash trucks are in the neighborhood, and we all know when the mail truck is here. But there is a lot of other stuff to keep track of, like the pesky meter readers. They are always messing with us. They come right to the fence and make their beeping sounds. The cable workers are here a lot too.

And man, last year was the worst. We had a big hail storm so every house had to have new woofs . . . I mean, new roofs. Man, those shingles are ruff . . . sorry. Each house they work on means three days of people talking and hammering on the roofs around us. That was difficult. All day I was in total alert mode. Crazy smells all over the place.

You never know when those strangers could come across the fence and do something that they would regret. I have to keep tabs on all that. I'm alert all the time. The humans don't see the danger and they don't listen to me near enough. There are a lot of things going on close around us that they just don't concern themselves with. If something did happen, I'm ready. They will be protected. Call me Protecto . . . Protecto the Great . . . Eagle Eye . . . Super Sniffer . . . Iron Paw . . . okay, Mango will do.

Tom's Perspective: There really is a since of peace knowing that Mango is here as security. She barks when something isn't right. She only barks when someone's at the door, a loud or strange noise comes from either outside or in, or she wants to play. We have no need for a doorbell. We know that someone is in our yard before they're ever near the door. She's our security system. A bad guy would not be smart to try and enter this house. She's a major part of our family; she gets a Christmas present every year. I have learned from Mango that God gives us security and sometimes in unexpected ways. With trust in God, we have the security that the most powerful force in the universe is watching out for us. He gives us tools, such as dogs, to help protect . . . if we don't teach them to stop barking.

4

Why Are Dogs So Special?

Five-year-old Cristian is saying his nighttime prayers before going to sleep. He has the greatest prayers, and I can hear them through the wall in Tom and Michelle's bedroom. When they put him to bed, they read a devotion or Bible story, say prayers, and then I take over. The best thing is to hear him call me into his room to stay with him at least until the last round of business in the backyard. Cristian wants me in there to feel protected. I run in and jump onto his bed, then lie down next to his feet. He is sometimes scared that bad guys will come into his room, and he knows I'll not allow that. It's one of the most special and needed feelings that I have. Sometimes I hide behind his rocking chair before bedtime to surprise him and be at the ready. He wants me there to protect him, and he knows I'll. I consider this to not necessarily be a job but an honor. I . . . am . . . important.

Humans don't usually give dogs a lot of credit. Since we don't speak English and we don't have thumbs, people believe we don't have intelligence and can't do much of anything. Seriously, we can do tons of things with just our paws and mouth: We can tear into a bone. We can perfectly arrange a blanket to sleep on. Some dogs can even open doors with their teeth. I haven't quite mastered that yet. But they have a little bell hanging from the doorknob going out back, and I ring that to inform them of my needs. Sure, it would be pretty cool to have thumbs, but that's not God's will. We do without. That in itself shows that when God does not provide, it sometimes is to show us that we can overcome.

Think about it, we can basically understand what humans are saying . . . but humans don't speak a lick of dog. A bark is an irritating noise to humans. They don't understand that barks have so many levels and meanings. Barks are dog words—things like I'm angry, I'm happy, I'm sad, I'm overjoyed, I'm nervous, I'm hungry, or a warning—something's wrong, alert, playing time, leave me alone, let me out to the yard, take me with you, lie down with me, *feed me* (which is different than just plain I'm hungry), my ball is stuck under the sofa, drop a piece of food on the floor *please*, don't forget to feed me, I don't need a bath right now, rub behind my ears, time for a walk, have you seen my chew toy, there's a rabbit out there, I *need* to go out this minute, unidentified stranger lurking in the front, and *feed me* or I'll tear up your underwear that I already have hidden behind the chair in the family room! Oh, there's more, but you get the idea.

This particular terribly smart and adorable dog can understand quite a few words. I don't understand everything my humans are saying, but I usually get the gist. I know their tone and I know their intention. I can understand a few words of their thoughts too. When they tell me to "go potty," I know what they mean and I do it on command, unless there's a stubborn streak going on that makes me rather persnickety.

The simple showoff orders like "sit and stay," no problem. "Go out." I got that. "Wanna bite?" That's an easy one. It doesn't always happen, maybe it's God turning the switch on and off, but I know when they're thinking about me and when they're going to have food for me. When Tom is making fruit smoothies, he gives me the unwanted pieces of apple. I know when it's time to walk in and be at his feet to get the goods. Before they even say something, I know they're going to feed me and I'm there at the ready.

God gives us dogs the strange power to know things about our humans to help them. We understand more than only words. We get feelings that help us know what is going on and how we can help. Sure, we can't speak a language that humans understand, but if they really try, humans can understand at least a little of what we're saying.

Our tails show our every emotion, our bark has various tones, and our body language speaks volumes. We are quite transparent. Every dog's communication patterns are unique, like humans. Your dog has his or her own way of talking, and food will always distract us . . . I mean, we *are* dogs, you know. Food always wins. We're always hungry.

Dogs are quite special and humans know that. They sometimes don't know the half of it, but let me get you started. Dogs can do some awesome things . . . normal, everyday stuff to me, but humans are amazed when they see some of our tricks.

Did you know dogs can predict earthquakes or sense a tornado or extreme weather when it's miles and miles away? Did you know dogs can sense a human's emotions . . . and we can tell when a human is hurt, inside or out? Of course, you know that we can hear pitches that humans cannot hear and we have far superior eyesight. We can find our way home . . . many times from a really long distance.

Did you know dogs can see angels? I have—a lot of them. And when I don't actually see them, I certainly smell them. Of course you know that dogs can find explosives and illegal drugs from across a room, but have you heard that some dogs can sense if a human has cancer or other life-threatening problem? Have you heard that some dogs can sense when a human with epilepsy is going to have a seizure? Have you heard that we can sense when a human has low blood sugar? We can alert our owners to take the right actions to correct that.

Dogs know when their humans are going on a long trip. You'll find us at the door waiting . . . so you won't forget to take us. We know when our humans are sad or anxious. We use our noses to figure out a lot of things. We can smell even subtle mood changes in humans. We know when to lie down next to our owners if they're feeling ill. For thousands of years, humans have used dogs to hunt, search, rescue, pull sleds, guide the blind, be a best friend, and so much more. What would humans do without us?

Take our feet . . . our paws blow away any old human feet. We can play in the snow for hours with no complaints; we can stand on hot pavement and not sweat it. Yet our paws are sensitive enough that humans can tickle them. All right, so we don't have opposing thumbs, but we do have opposing teeth and we know how to use them! And sure, we can speak English. You ask us what sandpaper feels like and we say, "Rough." You ask what is on the outside of a tree, and we say, "Bark." What does Tom look like first thing in the morning? "Rough, *rough!*" Face it, we're special.

Did you know that dogs are mentioned in the Old Testament of the Bible eighteen times? We must be important to be mentioned that many times. Think of the qualities that dogs have . . . and how closely we mirror the qualities of God. No wonder dog spelled backward is God. Unconditional love, infinite patience, an endless desire to please and help, and always positive and sure—these are only a few striking similarities that dogs try to mimic in the living God.

And yes, do not doubt it for a second, there is a God who created all of this, and He is real. Dogs show humans a tiny doggy door of what God is like. God gave us that wonderful job.

If you love God and you do things for Him instead of for yourself, you will be taken care of. Dogs understand this and live by it. Humans don't see it so clearly. They have to be shown again and again. Some humans get the miracles of God shown to them over and over and still don't recognize what He's doing. It drives me crazy, but many humans have so little faith.

Most of the time a human's anxiety is a result of a lack of faith in God. He gave us all these jobs to help humans and show them His unconditional love, patience, trust, and peace. Humans have to learn on their own or it's not genuine. God wants genuine, free will love and trust. Dogs are merely here to give an example of that . . . to help point humans in the right direction.

As I said before, food is a major stumbling block for dogs. In the wild, we dogs are always thinking about where the next meal will come from. So in a home, that thought is still strong in our minds. We are totally dependent on our humans feeding us. We know that because they're occupied with work, kids, and of course, feeding their own faces, some humans don't always remember us. Our stomachs always want food.

Rarely would we pass up anything we can eat. And even on major alert, food will take us out of the zone. If we fall down on the job or if we have bad manners, it's most often because of food. Whether it's something left on the counter or someone eating on the sofa who could easily drop a morsel, we'll likely forget what we're doing or lose sight of anything important.

I have accidentally scratched the top of my humans' feet because they dropped something and I ran to get it before they picked it up. We sometimes lose the focus of our jobs because of food . . . after all, we're not perfect.

Usually a squirrel or rabbit can distract us as well. Squirrels and rabbits are considered food at any level, at any time. God has His reasons for putting them here. I believe it's strictly for dogs to catch and eat.

I wish that humans would go to obedience school so they could learn how to talk to me and understand me more. Maybe they could learn some tricks too.

Here's my favorite new trick. Traditionally, our family uses the front storm door as a pulling device when a child has a baby tooth that is ready to come out. They tie one end of a string to the kid's tooth and the other end to the storm door. Sounds a little scary, but the kids love it. They stand back away from the door and then the child lets the door shut, pulling the tooth in the process. Once the door shuts, there's a tooth dangling at the end of the string.

They've done it for years, and the kids ask to do it. Cristian has done it for a few teeth, but yesterday was different. Cristian said, "I want Mango to do it!" Music to my ears . . . he wants me in on it! Of course, I've watched this before, but now I'm center stage.

They tied the string to Cristian's front tooth, which was barely hanging on. They had me stand in front of him, and tied the other end to my collar . . . I call it my necklace. Cristian had one of my favorite chew toys ready to throw. The plan was, I would take off at full speed and the tooth would come with me. Three, two, ONE—he threw my toy.

As planned, I ran at full speed. I awaited the cheering, praise, and accolades. My orders were complete . . . but they all just stood there. The string was still tied to his tooth . . . which was still in his mouth. The string had broken! Guess I don't know my own strength. I ran too fast and too hard. Okay, I was a little excited.

Luckily, they called me back to try again. This time, I had it down. A new string was tied, and ready I was. The chew toy was checked for excess slobber . . . occupational hazard. Now everyone was ready. I had the calm but firm run practiced in my head. I knew that a good fast trot would do it. That tooth was coming with me. Three, two . . . *one*! The toy was thrown . . . I ran before I even realized I was moving. Then I heard it, "Yesss! Look at that—*it worked.*" We *did* it! Maybe once the kids are all gone to college, I'll become a dentist. I mean, I can pull teeth with the best of them. All I need is my chew toy, and who needs pliers and pain deadening? This all happened before Cristian even knew the tooth was out, and he laughed and cheered the whole time. He was in control because he had the chew toy. This is definitely a new family tradition, and my job as a tooth puller seems to be secure.

Tom's Perspective: Okay, I don't believe our dentist has to worry about Mango becoming his replacement. We humans do not give dogs nearly enough credit, and we're still finding out surprising things they can do. Police use dogs, not only for their noses to sniff out drugs and bombs but also for protection and chasing bad guys. Dogs are used to help blind people have eyes and move about the world with more security. But most importantly, they're comfort for us. I have always had a dog, or dogs. I have always loved dogs . . . but through having Mango, I see that dogs are much more than companions, they're a God-provided source of therapy, hope, and peace that can easily be missed unless one chooses to look for it.

5

Did They Say Bath?

After being in the backyard for a while one morning, I give the usual paw scratch on the back door, wanting back in the house. I'd been outside for more than awhile since the weather was glorious and since we'd had some unwelcome visitors in our yard the previous night, I had to research and catalog every one of them. One smell in particular, though, is quite appealing but isn't from a rabbit, squirrel, or chipmunk. This is maybe from a bird or some other infrequent visitor whose smell needed to be duplicated.

This smell reminded me of how Michelle adds some kind of artificial smell before going out of the house. It isn't her normal smell, but it is certainly pleasing and makes me want to give extra sniffs to make sure I know her when she returns. I lie down and roll all over this smell that is in the ground. I really like it, and maybe it will disguise me from other dogs who knew my smell. If a human happens to visit our house and they bring a dog, then there might be instant attraction. I rolled it all over me, on my back of my head, and even on my beautiful and majestic tail. Proud was the only term that fit here.

These kinds of smells don't come along often. I smell good and no one can take that from me. It will likely last a few days and I will be well known for this special fragrance. So upon scratching at the door for reentry into the house, Michelle, who seems to have a higher sense of smell than many humans, yells with what I interpret to be envy and near jealousy. Turns out she pushes me back outside and yells, "What have you gotten into?" She yells even more convincingly, "You are *not* coming in until I give you a bath! That's disgusting!" Hmmm, I guess my definition of perfume and hers aren't quite the same.

I don't like baths. I *hate* baths. Baths were invented by cats and are likely illegal in some countries. I believe baths were used as a torture device in World War I. Baths are not necessary, and nothing good comes from them. Humans probably need them; dogs don't. Okay, it doesn't work that way, though. The cool smells I collect around the yard are fine with me, but my family won't let me live in the house with them, so I have to give on this one. I'll make my family chase me around the house and hide so they have to hunt me down before I'll surrender and let them take me to the tub. As we close in on the room where the tub is, my feet go in reverse mode. I would have a lot more success and a lot more traction if this weren't a hardwood floor. All you hear is the sounds of dog toenails wildly scraping across the slick wood. At this point, my legs are stiff and locked. If they want me in that room, they have to work for it.

Why do I hate baths? Easy . . . they're cold, and the running water is really loud when you have sensitive ears like mine. That noise scares me. Plus, the bath might lead to some other kind of torture . . . like cutting toenails or some other thing I could do without. When the water goes around my ears, my hearing gets all messed up; I hate that. Plus, the foam tastes like owl poop. I always try to be pointing toward the door because maybe, just maybe, they'll lean over and I can bolt . . . even though the door is closed.

My humans try to move back into place to get me in the tub, but I'm pretty strong so I don't make it easy. Again, all you hear is dog toenails scraping across a floor . . . only this time my nails are scratching against a wet tub. After a minute or two when I know that there's no toenail cutting or something really bad, I begin feeling a little better. Once I get settled down in the tub and feel the warm water, I kind of like it for a moment. I get rubbed and scratched and rubbed again, especially on my back. Oooo, yeah, right there. Wait, this is a bath we're talking about here. Have I gone nuts? I only have one real weapon, and I'm not afraid to use it. It's the dreaded shake. I sometimes will wait until whoever is giving me this forsaken bath is leaning down fairly close . . . maybe picking up hair that came off me (which also bothers me that hair is coming off). Wait for it . . . *shake*! Perfect . . . I douse them every time.

It's the only thing that makes baths any fun at all. It's quite wonderful. Hopefully, if all goes well, the bath giver is more drenched than the bath taker. Then once it's all done, I get out and get towel dried. For some crazy reason, that puts me in wacko mode. Once I get all scruffed up, I can't wait to run around the house like a wild dog. Every five or six pounces I have to try and shake all the water off. There's water in my ears, all over my tail, and under my arms . . . places the towel just doesn't work.

They try to stop me from shaking because it gets water all over the walls and floor, but that's half the fun. It's basically payback for giving me the bath in the first place. I like to see where I can get water marks. I have been able to get water almost to the ceiling . . . and I'll get it there one day. So maybe they don't like it, but it's a challenge that I have to take. It's just plain fun.

I'm not allowed to be in the house without being clean. As much as I hate baths, I know they're important to my humans. Thing is, I could survive fine without being clean. Besides my hair being in knots, it wouldn't matter . . . but it's important to my living in this space. In fact, when I remain clean for the sake of my owners, it makes me proud. It's all part of the package, I guess.

To live in this house, I have to follow the rules and stay clean. I can't help that my hair sheds everywhere; that's the part my humans have to worry about. No dog will clean his own hair . . . sadly, that's a trait cats do pretty well. It's not a dog thing. But we can try to stay clean, and accept that fact that our humans want to give us baths. It's the rules that apply in this home that I need to respect. If that makes the household happy, then I'm happy. That makes a happier home and a clean me.

> **Tom's perspective**: We are all dirty, so to speak. Being clean is certainly important to our physical health. But we're also dirty under our skin as well. There are things we do that make us feel dirty on the inside. When we open our heart to God, we feel a cleansing. God can and will take the dirt away and begin rebuilding a better you. Contrary to popular thought,

we don't already need to be clean for God to accept us. Sometimes people, when they hire house cleaners, clean their house before the house cleaners come because they're embarrassed of the condition of their home. God doesn't work that way, He already knows our condition; He simply wants us to come to Him. All He wants is our hearts. He wants us to be willing to be cleaner. Mango knows that in order to live inside our home, she needs to allow us to clean her. We need to allow God the same privilege. Cleansing allows us to experience a deeper, more meaningful relationship with our Creator. Now come on, Mango, time for another bath!

6

My Job of Pleasing

I wait for hours. It seems like days. There's a spot in the dining room where I can lie down and see out the front window. They leave the blinds high enough so I can see them drive up. I know they're coming home sometime soon. I could feel left out or angry that they left me here. Logic would tell me that I should be able to go pretty much anywhere with them. But I know better. They probably left me here to watch over the house or stay on the lookout for intruding animals in the yard. It doesn't matter. I'll love them when they get home. I'll shower them with licks and rub alongside of them no matter how long it takes. They took me in, they take care of me, and I'll never forget that. I'll be pleasing to them, and that's all there is to it.

Dogs are here to please humans, but more importantly, God. That's our job, day and night. In the same sense that we dogs were created to please humans, humans were created to please God. It's that simple. Just as there are some dogs who don't do their jobs well, they become selfish and lazy or mean and unproductive. Some humans do the same things. and don't remotely care about God. They don't try to please Him or love like Him. They don't acknowledge that He made all of this and everything is ultimately in His control. They don't even understand what God is trying to do with their lives.

These are sometimes the same humans who don't treat dogs very well. They don't treat us any better than they do the dirt on the floor. I have seen it and it makes me so sad. I heard many stories at the pound, er, uh, adoption center, that would make your tail curl. Humans can be terribly mean. And I know those types of people when I see or smell them.

There are humans who don't love God, who make their own rules and usually don't care much about others. Many times, those things go paw in paw. These folks don't usually have a purpose or direction for their lives, other than work. Things that are important to those humans have little real value. There's an empty void in them that nothing can seem to completely fill. They're always looking for something, but nothing seems to satisfy. They're searching for the next big thing. But that next big thing is never enough.

Humans try to win the lottery, which is nearly impossible, but they hold out hope in the lottery instead of for what the most powerful force in the universe can do for them. They want that big promotion, new car, or boat, and then a month later it isn't enough; they want something else to make life better. Now that's my perspective . . . from what I have experienced. These humans live for themselves. Sure, they help people or animals, but it's usually conditional, and the human gets upset and even hurt if the help isn't appreciated or, even better, reciprocated.

Those who have found the glory of God, the love and forgiveness of Jesus, have found unconditional and pure love, like the love shown to them by dogs. With God living in someone's heart, even the toughest, hardest heart softens. It's not that people become more compassionate in order to have God accept them; they become more compassionate because they have discovered the compassion and glory of God. They have hope. They know that someone loves and cares for them and that there is a real reason for their lives.

God radiates love, and it spreads quickly into a human's and a dog's heart. When a person opens his or her mind to the power and love of God, Jesus Himself will enter into the picture and start spreading compassion, peace, and hope. They don't change inside to accept God; they change because God gives them love and hope. Then the Holy Spirit of God lives inside their soul. When you believe, you get all three—God, Jesus, and the Holy Spirit—for the price of one.

The Holy Spirit heals, He helps, He teaches, He challenges, He comforts—He has wonders that most humans don't even understand. I can see in their faces when Jesus is lighting them up. All they have to do is open their minds to the fact that God is real, that Jesus, His true Son, lived, died, and is alive now, and everything changes. Hope becomes more commonplace and hearts become giving and less selfish.

Humans can shut this all off by letting pride take over their minds. It can happen fast. God doesn't leave, but humans seem to turn the volume knob down or tune Him out completely. God can be doing all kinds of things for a human, and one pawful of pride can mess it all up. Basically, trying to steal the glory from God is like grabbing the leash of an Irish wolfhound and attempting to push it instead of pull it. You go nowhere, neither of you has any direction, and both are left frustrated.

Our jobs are to please, no matter what the human believes, but a mean, uncaring human makes doing our job difficult. I have been there. I don't talk about it. Thank goodness they gave me up and I had a second chance. I'm not going to blow this one.

This family I have now loves God, and it shows in about everything they do. They have their moments, but God is pleased with them. That's why I'm here . . . God put me here to help them and to love them, to keep them pointed in the upward direction. Loving God is a choice. Loving Jesus is a choice. Being loving to an animal is a choice. Humans being loving to other humans is a choice. Being able to love is a gift. Being able to love God is a gift. Being forgiven through Jesus is a gift.

Some humans (and dogs) choose to leave these gifts unopened, but you never know what amazing things are in that gift box. How sad . . . it makes my tail droop. Some humans don't know that God desperately loves them and that He would do just about anything for them. They simply need to acknowledge Him and trust Him. Most dogs do that by instinct. Some canines have a cold heart—some hate; some don't love. But that is rare.

I haven't met many and haven't heard of many, but they're out there. I have seen a lot of selfish humans that don't care about Jesus and others. Wait . . . *squirrel*! I smell it . . . I feel it. This is wrong, way wrong. I go to the window; I see it! Get that thing, get that thing! *Get that blasted thing*! I bark, I scratch at the window, I try to even bump my head on the window to break through. Desperate times call for desperate measures. Yoof! Sorry.

Tom's Perspective: Mango is a pleaser . . . and most dogs are. They want us to know that they love us and will try most anything to prove that to us. Dogs can't communicate tough words, so telling us a simple, "I love you" is not available for them. We should re-member that words are not sufficient in many cases also. It's easy to say, "I love you; I care for you; I want to please you," but it is much more difficult to show it or try to prove it. We humans should *show* love, not simply try to *say* we love the ones we care for. More importantly, why can't we show, not tell, God that we love Him? We can show God our devotion by being a servant . . . by helping out our church in some way. We could offer to help someone before they ask for it. It's a serving attitude that reflects the loving ways of Jesus. Mango shows me a pleasing servant attitude every day, and I have learned from her that when you give yourself to others, it takes your own stresses and worries down a notch and removes the spotlight from your own troubles. Try it sometime; it's a life changer. Thanks, Mango.

7

I Don't Wish to Be a Human

I recently heard of a family who had a wonderful, loyal dog for many years. They were very attached to this wonderful family member. Who wouldn't be . . . I mean we are the best thing a family could have, right? The family had a young boy who had known the dog since he was born. The dog was very old and got sick. After a few months, the dog died . . . they finally lost their beloved family member who went on to heaven. The mother and father were worried that their son would be heartbroken, so they decided to make the occasion as special as possible. They had a funeral service in the backyard and invited many family members and friends. After the service, the mother and father sat down with the boy to talk about how he was feeling about everything. They began to talk about how dogs don't live as long as humans and were trying their best to explain the reasoning but came up short with any explanations. The little boy stood up and said, "I know why dogs don't live as long as we do. It's easy." The parents were startled and timidly ask him why. The boy proudly said, "It's because they learn to love a lot faster than people do."

Humans have it tough. I'm glad I don't have to deal with all they deal with. They have to have jobs and pay all kinds of money for things, and that seems stressful. These jobs occupy most of their time, and then sometimes they work when they're home. They say they need these jobs to pay for the house and the food. In some houses, both the mom and dad work. That makes for a slow day for us and a lot more stress when they get home.

Why humans can't just find their food and get by with a little shelter over their heads, I don't know. Dogs are the example of a simple life, and humans should take the hint. You don't need a lot of things . . . food, a roof, a chew toy or two, and most importantly, love. Everything else is extra. But I'll have to say that living in a house with heat and big sofas to sleep on is not so bad. Humans have to care for their children for eighteen or so years. That's a long time. That's longer than I'll live. We have to raise our pups for four or six months, and that's hard enough.

Of course, I'll never know the stress of having puppies because they broke me. Humans call it being "fixed," but I call it being broken, because nothing works. I can't have puppies . . . so it's all broken.

Humans have to deal with getting the food. I'm glad they do because then I don't have to find my own. I have never had to hunt, so I wouldn't be good at it. It would help my girlish figure, but from the looks of things around this neighborhood, there isn't much to eat out there in the wild. Only the wild dogs have to feed themselves.

Back in the day, years ago, wild dogs had to find their own food, but now more dogs live with humans and get handed their food. We appreciate that, and we hope our work is good enough to deserve the food we get, although neither animals nor humans deserve the things God has given us.

I'm certainly glad that we dogs don't have to deal with mowing the yard, painting the house, and washing windows. I think all that is silly and a waste of time. Looking for food and chasing a well-chewed ball . . . that's time used efficiently and productively. Some dogs are freaky afraid of vacuums, but I love them. I have to say that when Michelle gets out the vacuum, I rub up against her legs until she vacuums my hair. That is about the most amazing thing ever. That machine not only gets some of the itchy stuff off my back but it grooms me too.

Some humans don't know it, but we care about how we look. I mean, I don't want to wear silly clothes like some dogs do, you know . . . slippers and pajamas and such. But I do like to be brushed. This vacuum thing is the best thing, other than food of course. She takes the vacuum stick and scrubs my back and stomach . . . it cleans and takes out the old hair. Oh yeah, I shed—a lot.

Humans have to deal with a lot of things . . . some of which are not necessary to my food bowl. They have to go buy clothes . . . who needs clothes? Well, if you don't have any hair where it counts, I guess that makes a little sense. But all that stuff . . . mounds of clothes, come on. A whole room full of clothes. I can hide in that room for hours and no one will ever know. Tom has two poles full of clothes and Michelle has three. Why not just have a single coat that replenishes? Okay, humans were made that way and they can't help that they need something on them. But really, different clothes every day? And then stressing about not having the right thing to wear? Not for me.

Shoes . . . fifteen or twenty pairs of shoes, all those

shoes—who needs them? If they would walk on their feet for long enough, they wouldn't need shoes. If I wore shoes, then my feet would get soft and I couldn't go outside without them. Humans have so much stuff that they need to put it in places where they never use it. I really don't get that. Just make things simple!

They bring shoes home, and in a month, they're gone. Not gone as in given away or thrown away, but they're put in that strange room at the top of the house (I want up there; I hear noises up there), in a storage room, or in a closet. Sometimes I try to get stuff out of the closet when they leave it open. I try to remind them that they had it and they need it out again. Sometimes I get carried away and chew it up before I get it to them. I can't help myself.

Growing up, we don't get to be with our dog family usually; that's just the way it works. We get pulled away from our moms pretty early. We usually don't even know our dads. We get moved around sometimes, so we don't get attached to other dogs that much.

But when the person we're assigned to protect, comfort, and befriend goes away from this earth, it hurts. It changes our whole life—our purpose is gone, and our heart has a hole in it. Some dogs can't handle it and will grieve for a long time. Some dogs can recover and go for the reassignment. We all know that our human will be in heaven if they believed in Jesus . . . but not all of them do. That's sad. They're in for an eternity of hurt and anguish.

People worry about everything. They worry mostly about things that never happen. If people would believe that Jesus is real, if they would just understand that God is right there, then things would be so much easier for them. Dogs can see angels trying to help people believe and trust. Why can't they? They don't know who they're dealing with. When they pray, do they know they're dealing with the most powerful force on earth? When humans begin to mess with dark things . . . anything that opens a door to the bad forces . . . they're playing with fire. Fire can hurt.

Tom's Perspective: I'm not sure that dogs have it so easy, but they sure know how to deal with human-like problems . . . they simply blow their problems off. They move on. As a coach would say to his quarterback who threw a bad pass and the other team intercepted and ran for a touchdown, "Next play." The coach is telling the player, move on . . . you can't change it, you can't dwell on it. Dogs just move on. Dogs don't need much. They feel many of the same emotions that we humans feel, but they don't stress or worry over what has happened. Mango looks at me as if to say, "Next play, dude." I'm learning from her that worrying about the past is simply a waste of energy. You can't do anything about the past other than learn from it and do better on the next play.

8

The Devil's Bad Guys

Things are going fine while we're playing ball in the backyard. The whole family is out there and we're having a blast. Out of nowhere, I get a little excited and jump on Cristian and knock him over. He starts crying and is scared.

Tom says, "Get on up, Cristian; you're gonna be okay."

Michelle says, "No he's not, he's hurt."

Smiles turn to frowns and all of a sudden no one is having fun. Words are spoken that they will regret in a few moments, and darkness fills the air. They stop playing and go inside the house, and everyone goes their separate ways. Groans and huffs ware all I hear until about twenty minutes later when Cristian tries to rally everyone for a game of tag. No one budges until he and I start playing tug-of-war and the rest of the family joins in.

The devil won a small battle by waving his dark energy over the family and taking over the smiles for a short while. All he needed was a little anger to fuel the situation and then his dark emotions took over the family until the kid and the dog finally lightened the mood.

Dogs can tell when the devil's bad guys are around. And yes, they're around. The devil is nothing short of a liar, a mean spirited being full of hate and anger. Don't even give him an opportunity of entering your life because it will always turn out bad. His whole purpose is to pull humans and animals away from God. He has bad guys working for him—many of them. When they're around, things are just not right. Everything feels dirty and dark. Those guys try to make humans believe they're worth nothing. They try to make our humans be afraid and doubt everything that God stands for.

Fear is one of their most potent weapons, along with hopelessness and depression. When they attack Tom, he gets sad, scared, looks hopeless, and holds his head down . . . if he had a tail it would be tucked so far between his legs he would choke on the hair. He has these feelings that God won't help him, and he's alone in the battle of stress. He thinks, "Where is our God now?" Sometimes he buys into it and gets sad. When Tom gets sad and worried, he doesn't play with me like he normally does. I can tell when he's scared of the future and doesn't have the trust in God that he should have. The devil's guys try to make him believe he's worthless. He is not; no one is.

Tom is more impatient and always talks about how expensive everything is and that everybody is spending too much money. I know everything will be fine, but he doesn't. He gets so scared about money. He gets scared about keeping the house and being able to feed all of us. He feels so responsible for everybody. His business has been in trouble for over two years. But *every* month, God does something that saves the business. Why doesn't he get it? Every month Tom magically makes it through. We are all still eating and have a house.

God wants Tom's business to stay open. Tom tries to give God the glory and praise. He says he has given it up to God, but when he stresses, he takes it right back. God has been trying to show him that He is there. He comes in at the last possible moment, and when no other explanation will work, God makes it possible for the business to move forward.

Tom is starting to see it, but then all of a sudden, one little thing happens and he takes ten steps backward and stresses. When he begins to see the bone at the end of the tunnel, sometimes the lights go out and he's right back at hopeless again. It's simply a lack of faith, but I understand how he feels the stress. I'm working on him, but he needs to see that when you love God and trust Him, everything seems more tolerable. If I could just *talk* to him, he would understand. You see, having faith doesn't mean he doesn't doubt, it just means he's willing to turn to God and trust. God is there to help him know that he isn't alone, and God will redeem in His way.

It sounds silly, but try to take this in. Tom plays drums in the church band. I have heard it—the band is pretty good. Every week he'd worry about hurting his hands or doing something that would stop him from playing and helping the church. He'd be so afraid about not being able to play. But he doesn't remember that this service Tom is doing is strictly for God. He loves to serve in this way. He's using his talent that God gave him to be able to play music, and he uses that talent for God's kingdom.

Tom doesn't seem to understand that when you're doing something for God, God will make it happen. God will make a way for it even when a way doesn't seem possible. And God will usually give a layer of protection to those who are doing service for him. Tom has played in the church band for nearly seven years and has never missed playing at a service because he's hurt or sick. Even if he injures himself, the wound is miraculously better by Sunday. Tom has even told people about this, but he doesn't always believe it himself.

One day, Tom was up all Saturday night with an upset stomach. He felt awful, I could tell. He had no color in his face and looked like something I'd do in the backyard after eating something out of the trash. He couldn't find a substitute at that late hour, so he was going to either not show or play. Somehow at six thirty in the morning, he all of a sudden felt better . . . good enough to play in church. He left, played, and then came back home after church. Within an hour, he felt awful again and started throwing up. He was sick most of the afternoon . . . but he was able to play without a problem.

When God needs something to happen, it will happen. Tom is beginning to see that. If God wants this business to stay open, it will, as long as he's doing it for God and not himself, to make himself look good. If God needs you to do something, you'll be able to do it as long as you open yourself up to accept the challenge.

When the demons attack Michelle, she gets overwhelmed and feels like she isn't getting anything accomplished. That drives her crazy and she gets down on herself. The devil knows her weaknesses and her hot buttons. She doesn't realize that she doesn't have to do a hundred things a day to be successful. The demons make her feel like she's a failure and a bad mother. I try to help her feel worthy, but there's only so much a dog can do in that department. She's a loving and caring mom and does better than anyone I've ever seen. I wish I could tell her that.

The devil is pretty crafty when humans are lonely. Some say that loneliness is the devil's playground. That's when a human's mind goes in fifty different directions. Dogs can handle loneliness pretty well. We can sit or lie down all day, waiting for our humans to come home. Usually, I can hang with the best of them, but there are moments when I have to find something to chew. My mind, though, is fine. I don't sit there and think that my humans are not ever coming home—some dogs get a little wacky like that. Bella, the Chihuahua down the street, will chew up all kinds of things.

I don't worry unless I see suitcases. Then I get a little crazy . . . I try every trick to get outside and catch a ride with them. Dogs can get panic stricken. But that's usually only after their humans pack and leave for a long time. That's when someone else comes in to feed us, and we don't see our family for a while. Dogs usually know when their humans are going to leave for any length of time. I'm lucky in that department; my family usually takes me with them on trips. They have this big camper thing that we all pile into.

Dogs are especially good at helping humans with loneliness. That's when we shine, if the humans let us. But when they deal with someone dying, our job gets really hard. Michelle's mother, Paulette, is very sick and is probably not going to live. She's a dog lover. The last time I saw her, I knew she was sick . . . I could tell. I knew this sickness was something that had been in there for a long time and had taken the healing power inside her body and made it weak. Whenever she comes to our house, I know she has a good, spirit-filled heart. I know she loves dogs.

That makes a big difference in a person's life, by the way. When people treat an animal with respect and love, then their hearts are much closer to the way God prefers. How do I know? Dogs hear God. We hear with our sixth or seventh sense . . . I can't remember which. It's either our sense of reading humans' minds or hearing God. We know what He wants and what is supposed to happen, and if humans don't listen or follow, then things don't always turn out so well. We can usually tell when something strange or odd is going to happen. If humans would watch us more closely, they would get a hint of some of those things. God knows everyone's hearts. He and His angels not only read minds, but He reads feelings. He can tell when humans are honest even with themselves and when they're hurting inside. We know it too.

Like Michelle . . . she loves her mother, and she's nervous that her mother won't get better. I know she's nervous too. She has a lot on her mind and has a shorter fuse than usual. She needs a big lick on the side of the face. I can't always get her down to my level, and she won't always let me on the sofa with her when she's upset. But I bark and rub against her side. Sometimes I grab her hand with my teeth . . . oh, not hard, of course; just a nibble. But she understands and pats me. She thinks I want to go out. I know she's worried about her mom hurting so bad and dying. She knows about heaven and has the great comfort of knowing that her mom will go there.

I know that Michelle will miss her mom. Humans worry so much about missing people. I sense, though, a peace within her . . . she knows that her mom will be in heaven and she'll see her again. She knows that the pain will be gone and her mom will be in complete paradise.

Humans have to see God on their own. If they choose to see God, then they find comfort. They know that they will see their family again. All they have to do is believe. I'll help Michelle. She believes . . . I know that, I sense those things. She's sad because her dad is going to have a hard time with it, and she doesn't want to watch her mom go through the pain. Dying is a tough thing. Sometimes God pulls them right up to heaven, and sometimes He gives them or their family members time to patch things up.

God has His reasons. He makes the rules. He made this place; He knows how things have to be. I don't ask questions. When I do, sometimes I don't understand the answer. Too much for me . . . back to chewing my nylon bone.

Humans will not always choose to see God, especially in tough situations. That's sad, because God usually won't just jump out in front of them and say, "Here I am . . . don't you see Me now? Here . . . here's a big, bold miracle . . . see Me now?" God doesn't play that way. You have to choose to see Him first. Then He'll show Himself in all sorts of ways. Dogs don't have to choose that . . . we get to see what He accomplishes, and we get to see His angels sometimes.

Sometimes they're invisible, but the visible ones have the most beautiful colors and a strange glow around them. We see them; humans don't. Sure dogs don't see colors very well but we see the amazing colors of angels. Angels are so common that we dogs don't get startled by them or bark at them. Once in a while, I'll lift an ear. We have this understanding . . . angels have their work, and we let them go about their way. Sometimes I still lift my head and stare, but for the most part, I don't get in the way. It's fun to watch.

The other day, an angel stopped Cristian from walking into the countertop corner. At his height, he would have had a direct hit in the middle of his forehead. It would have left a good-sized hole for a few days. Instead, the angel made him trip and fall a few feet short of the countertop. He fell down, didn't get hurt at all, and ran off into the other room. Humans would never know that the angel did that. They would have just thought that he tripped and fell. At five, he doesn't have the best balance in the world anyway. Humans don't choose to see that kind of stuff at all. Angels are all around and they really help us all out. They remain anonymous and, most of the time, humans never know they're there.

Tom's Perspective: Mango looks off into space with a serious and inquisitive look far too often. If it's not an angel or something of the dark side, I don't know what else it could be. Why not? They see, hear, and smell things that I don't all the time. I have learned from Mango that God is closer than we think. He's not just watching from a distance. He and His workers (angels) are always doing things for us— guiding, protecting, nudging, giving us feelings of self-worth and meaning, and we don't know it most of the time. Just the same, the devil and his evil minions are trying to make us feel angry, sad, depressed, lonely, and worthless.

The beautiful thing is that God's side is more powerful than the other, and if we not only believe in God, but *believe* God, we can beat the sadness, worry, stress, and worthlessness every time. God is bigger and more powerful than any problem we can face. God is bigger than problems at work, than the people who gossip about us, than the money we owe to people or banks, than the sickness or the worries that tomorrow might bring. Mango shows me the power of being positive all the time. She's a happy, loving, full-of-life being that knows there is life beyond the worry. She shows me that I can believe God and life a much happier life.

9

We All Have Choices

Right now I'm in the area where the family eats their food; they call it the breakfast table. They have a dining room, but they never eat there. It seems like that table is for stuff that the kids bring in after school and such—papers, backpacks, tennis rackets, you get the picture. Anyway, they're getting ready to eat. Older sister Carolyn is visiting, and she brings her plate of food over to the table and sets it down. She goes back to the kitchen to get a drink, and now the plate is sitting there all by itself with no one guarding it. I try to make a move to grab what I can off the plate. Tom yells at me, "Mango!" And then there it is—the point. When he points at me, I know I have done wrong, either I have or am about to make a bad choice. When he points at me, I freeze and try to think over all the available choices . . . none at this point even come to mind, and I simply freeze and hope he doesn't send me out of the room. When we have a staring contest, he'll win at that as well, because when he stares at me and doesn't look away, I feel embarrassed like I've done something wrong . . . even if I haven't. I don't like the stare off, and I surely don't like the *point*. And if I get the *point* and *stare*, then I need to hit the floor and act wounded.

One of my favorite activities is riding in the car. Whenever Michelle or Tom gets ready to leave the house, I'm at the front door ready to go with them. I'll sit on my back paws and look my most beautiful, and I'll give them my "I reeeeeeally want to go with you" look. If you have a dog, you probably know what that looks like—tail wagging, perfect smile, looking up at just the right way to where I look like a trophy dog. No one could resist this face. They take me sometimes, and when they do, it's the greatest thing since chewable socks. They have a big car, so I can ride in the back or I can lie down in a seat. As long as I get to go with them in the car, I don't care where we go or how long I have to wait when they go inside some place.

One day, I made a bad choice. They were leaving the house to take Chloe to school and they decided to take me. When they open the door and say, "Come on, girl," that's my cue. They don't put a leash on me because I always go straight to the car. I might take a detour for a moment, but when they open the back gate of the car, I run to it and jump in. The door opens with a button, so sometimes it opens more slowly than I think and I hit my head on the bottom of the door before it opens enough. I hate that, but I still would rather have the hurt than miss the ride.

On this particular day, all went as planned. I looked perfect and ready to go. I'm sure I was irresistible, and only a nonfeeling stack of dry dog food would have passed me by that day. It must have worked because they gave the cue and I went outside. All of a sudden I smelled something. It was not a smell that normally hit me when I went out the front door. It was a squirrel, and it needed to be found. It wasn't far because the smell was strong. It was quite easy to find . . . it couldn't hide from this nose. It was in the bushes in the house next door! I headed over to show it who had seniority around there. The moment I got there, it ran. "Not on my watch, you don't!" I barked. "You might just be today's breakfast!" It wouldn't stop or run up a tree. I ran and ran, with Tom and Michelle yelling and running after me.

At first it seemed like they were backing me up, chasing the squirrel with me. I liked their spirit and attitude . . . until I realized they were yelling at me. By that time I'd run so far I was not sure how to get home. Bad choice. I knew better. Now this nose had to get me home, because I was not going to leave my family to be on their own. Worse yet, I wasn't going to allow them to get a different dog.

I put my nose into high sensitivity mode. I could smell it—home. I can smell it more near trash day because there are smells of home in those cans, and they travel pretty far. I can't believe they traveled this far, but I'm glad they did. I ran toward home and found Tom and Michelle, who were quite upset because they couldn't find me. I broke their trust of letting me go outside without a leash. Worse, I made them late in taking Chloe to school.

This is when I first heard the word "grounded" associated with my name. "Mango, you are grounded!" they yelled. Grounded? Me? You're kidding, right? I'm the house favorite . . . everybody loves me. How could they possibly ground me? I see every kid in the house get grounded. They get their cell phones taken away, they can't go to social events or football games, they get sent to their rooms. But me . . . what would they ground me from?

Oh, I get it . . . I can't ride in the car. Darn. It took weeks before they let me go with them again. Every time I sat at the door and looked my best for them to take me, all I heard was, "Mango, you're grounded." I felt like a human teenager—one that wants to yell back and say it wasn't my fault. But it was. I was mad . . . but mostly at myself. I have to work on self-control. It was a bad choice . . . a really bad choice. I'll think a bit harder before I chase a squirrel more than an earshot away from home. It was my choice and I blew it.

I'll always choose to play tug-of-war. That's the best part of the day. See, we get it right . . . always keep it light, make sure that fun is always part of the plan. Tug-of-war is not just mindless playing; it's therapy. It keeps the stress in check. Have you ever seen a stressed dog? There are many. If you have, play tug-of-war with him; it'll help you both.

Humans begin messing that whole theory up at about age twelve. What is it about middle school that makes them too serious? God doesn't want humans to be so serious. He wants them to have fun, He wants them to choose to see Him, trust Him, and just have fun. He wants them to stop worrying so much and to trust that He can handle things. It's going to be okay! Play tug-of-war. I have a short rope that's perfect for it. You should have one too.

If tug-of-war isn't your thing, then find something that's not serious and make it your thing. Make it something childish and playful . . . something that takes you away from your stress. Humans, dogs . . . even silly cats need childish distractions. We have the luxury in this house of a five-year-old who loves to play. Playing is his life. Sometimes the other humans in this house will stop and play with him . . . that helps their stress almost immediately.

I believe God put this beautiful adopted boy here to show them that He wants everyone to be like a child . . . to believe like a child, play like a child, trust like a child, smile like a child with nothing hidden behind it, and love everyone like a child. That doesn't mean we shouldn't have concentration and careful focus . . . I concentrate on plenty of things.

Food comes to mind. My humans need to concentrate on their schoolwork, their jobs, or child raising. But they should never take it so seriously that they lose sleep over it or stress to the point where they don't want to play tug-of-war. That's when God gets disappointed. When those humans get so wrapped up in stress, then they surely don't think God can help them.

If they only knew what God does to make things work out. If they only knew what God does to keep them safe. Sure, I warn them of things going on around them, but God makes things happen or not happen . . . whether the humans believe He's there or not. My humans believe in God and they love Jesus, but they still stress—a lot. I have to work on that.

They choose to stress. It's a choice. God says that stress and worry make Him sad. It means they don't trust that God has a reason for everything, and *He* doesn't make mistakes. He wants humans to trust that He will make everything all right. Through situations and difficulties, humans grow and learn.

No human has ever learned from being comfortable and untested. God wants them to learn, and He wants them not to worry about the next day or the next week. They can't do anything about next week . . . and their worrying sure doesn't change anything.

God is already working on next week. Tom doesn't see that right now. I see worry in his face . . . he's a worrier. I see the Holy Spirit in him. There is a glow around him that is trying to comfort him. The Spirit lives in all my family. All kids have it, and any human who believes in Jesus has it. They don't use it much, but they can. I see it trying to calm them, heal them, and teach them. They have to open their hearts to it and listen. Angels are always around trying to help them too.

I try to comfort Tom and take his mind off the stress. I surely don't have the power of the Spirit or angels, but he can see me and I can do things physically that will distract him and love him. We are making headway because he used to get really upset and stressed about everything. Now he smiles more, but it's still taking a toll on him. He still comes home with problems from work . . . mostly money problems. People aren't paying him or he lost a project or new ones aren't happening fast enough. He owes a lot of people money and he can't always pay them on time. He worries about being able to pay his employees or make loan payments. He chooses to stress over it and worry. Doesn't he know that worry is a waste of time and energy?

As a dog, I can't put myself in his place and say I wouldn't stress because I just don't stress. I see the things that are going on all around. If he could only know that God is helping him so much. God is making tomorrow work. Why does he stress about tomorrow? He can't change it at all.

Another thing humans have a choice in is patience. One of my jobs is to teach patience. God gives all dogs that job. Every night, last thing before bedtime, Tom takes me out for one more check of my Pee-mail. And every night, I make it hard for him to find me. Sometimes I hide in the upstairs bathroom, sometimes behind the weight set in the bonus room. Sometimes I hide in the sun room, and sometimes under the dining room table where he has to bend over to see me. It teaches him patience. Some nights he has patience and isn't upset by the time he finds me, but some nights he's quite upset. When he finds me, I lie there as if I'm asleep and he has to pull me up. I like that attention.

I have a place where I hide at least twice a week. It's under an old radio with legs that connect at the bottom. I lie down with my legs entangled between the radio's legs. When he comes to get me, he has to pull me up, but it's harder because my legs are tangled in the legs of the radio. He can't pull me out without having to untangle my legs. It takes a few minutes before he can free me, and sometimes, when he gets a few of my legs out and starts working on the next ones, I play dead and secretly put the other ones back into place, tangled in the radio legs. It's humorous and quite funny. He chooses to get angry most every time I do this, but he is improving slowly. I'll break him. When people pray for patience, God doesn't give patience . . . He teaches it. Humans have to choose to learn it. Think of this: God provides the wind, but humans have to raise the sail.

Humans also have to choose to be compassionate. God gives compassion to all humans, but they have to choose to use it. To have compassion, you have to put yourself in the other animal's (human's) place and ask yourself—would I enjoy having that done to me? Or, what if that situation happened to me, what would I want another to do for me? What would help me the most if I were in that animal's position? Excuse me . . . woof, bark, bark, arff hmfff . . . sorry, it was a rabbit.

God gave every living being choices. He didn't create robots. We're presented with situations and given a choice of how to deal with them. It's a lifelong quest . . . we continue to receive new challenges. Humans get angry or scared by the situations they're put in—they usually just want out of the situation instead of trying to handle it and learn from it. The learning process involves understanding that it's not what happens to us that's important, but how we handle it. We can either choose to get angry or to deal with it.

God never makes mistakes, and He's orchestrating everything . . . kind of like, what do humans call it . . . a conductor. The conductor is in charge and leads the musicians as a group. If the players rely on the conductor, then they only have to deal with what they're to play and nothing else. If they start worrying about what's on the next page or what the other player is doing, they get distracted and might mess the song up. Let the conductor worry about that.

If we get angry or scared at a situation, then we believe that God has made a mistake and we shouldn't be in this position at all. Why did that happen to me? I didn't do anything to deserve this! Why me? Humans should instead ask: Why *not* me? What did we do to *not* deserve this?

It's not about you! It's always about God. We can never do enough for God. We can't outgive Him or do enough to lift up His kingdom. The blessings we receive are gifts from Him simply because He loves us. He doesn't make bad things happen, but He doesn't always stop them for our learning or for our betterment. We see a problem as a burden; He sees it as an opportunity. We see bad things as negative and scary. God sees them as a chance to grow and become stronger. We would never choose for ourselves to go through a hardship. God knows that and puts us in positions to grow. He doesn't make mistakes, and He sees the ultimate goal and possibility of each challenge and what we can learn from it. He never says oops.

We believe we know what is best for us, when we basically know nothing and have no idea what we *really* need for our growing and well-being. When bad things happen, we think they're awful and we may never see the good in them. God will always make good of bad if we allow Him to take the credit and glory.

God does see the good, and we need to embrace the fact that if we allow Him to make things good in our lives, we'll be totally fulfilled. Where God takes us is always good in the long run. When things are out of your control and you can only watch what happens . . . God is there. He is working, and if you believe He is there for you and loves you then just be patient and allow God to be God.

Thank Him for the blessings you have had on this day. Choose to see His gracious blessings. No matter what, your situation could be worse. Make the choice to allow God to do His thing. The burden of fear and anxiety will nearly disappear. Choose to see His wonders; dogs see them all the time. We take the time to watch and be thankful.

Tom's Perspective: We all make bad choices. God knows that. We can dwell on the bad choice or we can learn from our mistakes and move on. This world can be a bad place because of people's bad choices. As hard as God tries to stop people's bad choices, He also gave them free will and allows them to do what their hearts tell them. We all wonder why bad things happen. Nine out of ten times, those problems resulted from someone's bad choice. It isn't necessarily our job to fix other people's mistakes, but it's our job to spread the hope and love of Jesus. If we live with the strength, power, and hope of Jesus, then we can go forward with more confidence. Life is like driving at night . . . you can only see as far as the headlights shine and no farther. You can't see much of anything behind you, and you can't change where you've been anyway. When you try to turn the light on inside and figure out what's going on, you get blinded and you can't see anything around you. Have the faith to keep moving in high gear. *Floor it!*

10

Want Fries With That Shake?

Did you hear, I hate baths, but one of the perks of a bath is what happens immediately afterward. Last week, at the end of a lengthy and torturous bath, Tom turned off the water. Before he could grab the shower curtain, before he could back away, before he could grab a towel for protection, I shook and shook. If he's going to keep me in here and wash me, he's going to wear some of this water with me.

Shaking is reserved for animals. Humans can't do it well. We shake for a few different reasons: to soak our humans after a bath or after a good rain. It lets them know that we like to share, that we're able to dry ourselves, and that it's time to lighten up a little. We shake because we have hair that needs to be straightened or removed. When you have a thick coat of hair, sometimes you just need to get rid of some of it. Sometimes it takes a shake to straighten our collar.

When Tom tries to shake, he calls it a dance . . . it's not pretty. When he does it, the whole family asks him to stop. Now the girls, they can shake . . . er, uh, dance. They even have dance games that they play. I try to jump up on them and shake . . . dance with them. It still doesn't get their hair fixed like the way I shake, but I give them points for trying.

Most of the time, our collar is all the clothes we have, so it's important. Sometimes this collar gets turned upside down or simply itches. A good shake will correct things quite quickly. We also shake because things can get stressful in a hurry and we need to shake the stress away. Shaking our problems away really works. We can shake and move on. Problems are gone, and we move on to the next challenge or nap, whichever comes first. Shake it off.

Tom's Perspective: I really wish I could shake like Mango. I have tried over and over and I don't have what it takes to shake like a dog. Not only would it help after a shower, but I could learn from Mango to shake off the stress that can develop so quickly. We can, however, mentally shake off problems. After we have tried our best to handle a situation and then have given the result to God, we should just shake it off and let it go. Likely, our hair won't go flying unless, of course, it's really long, but we can lessen our worry a bit by shaking things off.

11

Listen to Your Dog's Intuition

I'm in the kitchen and Michelle is preparing a meal . . . dinner it seems, since it's later in the day. I have a sense that she will drop a slice of carrot before long. The kitchen floor is my territory. When food is dropped, it's mine. No matter what time of day it is, whatever ends up on the ground will disappear and the floor won't need cleaning. One of the toughest things to swallow is when they beat me at my game—when something is dropped, and they pick it up and clean it before I can get to it. I'm sure in some countries that's a community service offense. Beating me to the dropped food can be construed as animal cruelty if done often enough because I sometimes hit my head on a cabinet running toward the other side of the kitchen.

I'll hang out right under her to be able to snag that carrot before she can bend down and pick it up. Like now when she's talking on the phone, and I can tell she's only half watching what she's doing. I'm watching more than she is. Usually I let my looks entice her. I mean, that's all I have. I sit and look my sweetest (which is pretty barking sweet). I have my ears propped up just so and my head cocked to one side. Irresistible, I'm sure. If possible, I'll lick her hand as she walks by. That is a surefire way to get noticed and get a little handout.

You see, there are many approaches to get the goods. This time I'm lying down in the middle of the floor, right around her feet, so she has to step over me to go to the fridge. Usually that makes it even harder for her to hold on to food. Here it comes, wait for it . . . wait for it. Score! A cucumber slice . . . always a good appetizer. And there will be more. How do I know? I just do. I'll be taken care of. Some call it intuition . . . I call it instructions from God's Spirit. He talks to us even about scoring food. We just have to listen. He tells us—dogs and humans—all kinds of things, especially when we're about to do wrong.

Michelle has good intuition, or more accurately, she listens to the Spirit more often than many. Women usually do. But Michelle really has it. She's wise. I've heard humans talk about women's intuition . . . women tend to use the sense God gave them to be more in tune with the Spirit. They hear God talking to them more often than not.

I wish Tom would listen to Michelle more often. She tells him many Spirit-led things, and he doesn't always give her credit for her intuition. Whenever he makes a decision about the business without involving her, it hardly ever goes the way he wants. He doesn't stop and pray about the decision and doesn't ask her advice. That usually ends up badly. Michelle prays often about decisions and listens to the little feelings God gives her. She's in tune with her spirit and acts when God gives His nudges.

Tom is learning because I hear him saying that he should have asked her or listened to her advice. One of these days, he'll learn. Really, most guys are in this same position. They don't give the women close to them credit for their guided intuition. Guys, take heed—God put women here to help. He gave women a close connection with His guidance.

The thing is that everybody who believes in Christ automatically has the Spirit inside them and can receive His guidance. Most human males are too proud to listen. I mean, they don't even ask for directions, much less listen to the God-powered Spirit inside them. The Spirit knows everything. He's part of God, so of course He's going to know the best decision for us. When you hear the word intuition, it's really God talking. Just listen.

Tom's Perspective: The hardest thing for me to do is admit I don't know everything . . . that someone might have a better way and I might be wrong. The way Mango submits to what we want from her is enlightening. She somehow knows that we want the best for her, and even taking her to the vet, as much as she hates that, is ultimately good. When the doctor is taking her temperature, in the only place they take a dog's temperature, or when they're treating her for something, she looks up at us as if to say, "I guess you know what you're doing . . . I don't like it, but I'll sit here and take it because you love me."

If we can look to God and say the same thing, then our problems become easier to endure. I have learned from this nutty dog that I shouldn't let myself be overcome with worry . . . things that are happening have a much deeper purpose and reasoning than I can see at the moment. If I simply look beyond the feelings of fright, helplessness, hopelessness, and self-centeredness to see the bigger picture God is painting, then problems are not only more acceptable but they can help me. Mango has helped me learn that submitting to your master has huge, positive benefits.

12

Stop That Butt Sniffing

My family gets so embarrassed. When someone comes to visit our house, I have to check them out. I mean, I'm the security department here. No one makes it past security until they pass inspection. One day a lady came to visit our house, even after I attempted to bark her away. I stick my nose by her to do my security check, and they pulled me away before I could ever get started with my full body check. How am I to do any quality work when I'm stopped in my tracks?

Dogs sniff butts . . . that's simply a fact of life. Get used to it. Humans don't like it. They don't understand it. It's how we dogs understand one another. We can sniff another dog's butt and know most everything we need to know about them. I can get all I need to know in usually five sniffs . . . sometimes six. I call it my background check. That takes all prejudgment out of the picture. Humans certainly don't have the smelling power to do that, nor would they be caught dead sniffing a butt. But they need to, in a different way of course.

Humans simply use their eyes to look at a person and draw conclusions. Humans should learn to sniff butts, so to speak. They need to take time to learn about a person before trying to figure out on their own who the person really is. Humans will look at people, sometimes just at the color of their skin or the clothes they're wearing, and make a judgment about them. They look at the car another human drives and have instant feelings about them . . . a total prejudgment.

Tom used to drive a twenty-year-old junker car. He paid very little for it. It was way out of the cool zone . . . not a car that would deserve a second look. He drove it because it was cheap and it got him to work and back. He used to talk about the looks he would get from people in the next lane. It was as if his junker were in the way and their expensive cars made them feel like they were someone special.

He now drives a twelve-year-old truck because he carries a lot of TV stuff around. It has hail damage and isn't all that pretty, but he doesn't mind. If someone judges him because of how his car looks, then let them judge. It's their problem, not his. How can you judge a man inside a car when you haven't met him? A dog won't draw a conclusion on another dog without butt sniffing first. Think about this, if Jesus were here today, what kind of car would He be driving?

Protection mode is different. If we see another dog, we'll warn our humans that a dog is close by. Humans think we're barking at that dog because we don't like it, but it's simply a warning to our humans and to the foreign dog. Once we get to sniff, then we'll see if things are acceptable.

I have noticed that many Christian humans aren't as quick to pass judgment on other humans as quickly as others, but judgment still happens. Humans are judgmental beings, but they can choose not to be. They can choose to look at another person, knowing that God loves that person or animal as much as He loves you. No more and no less.

He loves the homeless guy, the ruthless banker, the do-nothing freeloader, and the pro-life activist all the same. I see all those people on TV, and I know that God loves them *all*. Some Christians—and dogs know if people are Christians—get defensive or nervous when they see someone dressed in ragged clothing as if they had no home. Some get pompous or angry when they see someone with a different skin color. How can a skin color or country of origin make a person any different? They're people and that's all there is. Judging someone because of their skin color or race is more ignorant than a sheep . . . and sheep are, well, stupid. I have been to a farm with the family and I sniffed some sheep butts. Stupid has a certain smell, and sheep have it.

My humans are not judgmental, but even they have times where they're nervous about someone or they think a person looks dangerous or mean. They should let me sniff it out and check instead of depending on their eyes to check a person's intentions. They shouldn't assume that a person has bad motives, unless a dog is not around. Without a dog, they should be guarded but still not judgmental.

My humans will usually stop and give money to people with signs on the side of the road at red lights. They will talk a little to them, but when the light turns green, off they go. I know that some people won't even stop. Why? Because of prejudgment . . . some humans believe that people who say they're homeless are scamming. They believe these people are just out trying to get money from idiots who don't care who they give money to.

How does God feel about that? I say He feels like it's not your responsibility what those people do with the money. He wants humans to give their money to others in need with a cheerful heart. They shouldn't even be concerned with what anyone does with the money. It's a sharing attitude that we need to adopt. We are all here to help others. That's what dogs do. We give our all to help humans without regard to our own selves. We give without judgment and without care what they do with our gifts.

Take time to get to know others. Most of the time, humans have a good nature about them. They may not look on the outside like how they feel on the inside. When humans are stressed, they have a different appearance. That alone can make people look like they don't want to speak or offer help, when inside they're wonderful people.

Humans don't know what has happened to another person in the last hours, days, or months. They don't have a clue about what has affected people to put them in a bad mood or make them forgetful or unwise. Don't assume their reactions are personal or an attack on you. Have some compassion. Realize they might be having a bad day. Smile and love them into having a better day. That's what dogs do all the time. If humans could do that a little more often, there would be a lot more leftovers.

Tom's Perspective: This is a real takeaway from Mango. Why are we humans so prone to judge others? It happens to the best and worst of us. Sure, dogs approach others dogs cautiously, but they don't like or dislike until information has been collected. I don't have an interest in sniffing anywhere on another person, but I have learned from Mango that we can all spend a little more time asking questions and getting involved with people enough to know some history before judging them. The more we learn about other people and their problems and issues, the more we realize that others are going through the same, if not worse, situations than us. Once we let down our walls a little, we might be able to help that person in some way. Helping someone through a problem like a job loss, divorce, or the loss of a loved one helps us not to concentrate on our own problems and helps pull us out of chronic worrying.

13

Speaking of Buts

Sometimes we go visit a dog park here in town. Dog owners take their pride-and-joys to a fenced-in area to let them run and play with other dogs. As fun loving and sporty as I am, my humans are nervous that other dogs might see me as, well, a little too excited. My family tries to take me only when there aren't a lot of dogs at the park. We have, on occasion, turned around and driven home when the park was overcrowded with dogs. When they do allow me to go to the park, after they have told me to be calm and reserved, I, of course, run like crazy and meet as many dogs as possible in the first thirty seconds. The only problem with that is I have a lot of butts to remember. As we've already established, sniffing butts is how dogs prejudge and get acquainted with one another. The dog park simply has too many butts for me to take in. Humans don't remember names very well. I guess I have a problem remembering butts.

If you ask me, humans have more than one but. Actually, most humans have many buts, say like two or three hundred buts. Sometimes they have that many buts in one single day. You ask, what am I talking about? I constantly hear humans say, "I would do this it or that, but . . ." They would take me to the dog park, but . . . They would save the world from mean and uncaring cats, but . . .

There always seems to be a "but." Buts get in the way of nearly everything a human dreams. If they want to spend time with their kids, there's a but. If they want to play fetch with the dog, there's a but. "But I have to wash the car, but I have to do the bills, but I have to take a nap, but I have to work"; they always have a but.

So much could get accomplished in this world, *but* . . . Humans all have dreams, exciting dreams, except many of them halt with the word but. It's like saying, "Sit and stay till playtime is over." Many times those dreams come directly from God speaking inspiring, motivational thoughts through his Spirit to the "but" sayer—things that will take them a step further in growth and strength. These inspired thoughts turn into ideas, which turn into lifelong dreams, which turn into great things that can affect many people. But those dreams get squashed by a single yet very powerful "but." Procrastination and fear can stop the greatest of dreams and be disguised as a "but." All humans need to not do something is to have a "but." There is usually something that prevents them from doing something great.

Satan has powerful tools to stop our fulfillment and journey toward God. He uses fear, worry, self-doubt, procrastination, and diversion. The word "but" can help out in each of these excuses.

If you look at the anatomy of any living being, their butt is not only something that can't be seen, but it always lags behind. Really, you can't see your butt. It also gets sat upon all the time. Don't let your but get in the way of something great and powerful. When you have something you feel you need to do, if it is something you feel God is tugging at your heart to do or something that would please God, don't let a simple "but" stop you. Go after your dreams and those little heart tugs. You never know where those will take you. In other words, scratch the itch that may very well be on your . . . well, you know what I mean.

> **Tom's perspective**: I cannot count how many times I almost did something great, only to be slammed into the brick wall called "but." I seem to be able to talk myself out of a lot of things simply by letting "but" get in the way. Mango, on the other paw, just does things . . . without even thinking. Her life and ways are simple. She doesn't worry and she doesn't wait for all the pieces to come together before she acts. She sees a toy, she pounces on it like a cat. She chews until it is in pieces and totally believes that I'll purchase another one. And she's totally correct.

14

Let's Play Some Fetch

One day, Tom and I were playing fetch with an old cloth soccer ball. Until I bit a hole in it, it was my favorite toy. He would kick it high in the air and I would beat it to the place where it would land. Twice it hit me on the head when it landed. One time Tom kicked it over the top of the play set, which has a little fort over the top of a sandbox. The fort has a ramp going up to it on one side and an opening with a ladder to reach the fort on the other side. When Tom kicked the ball way over the top of the fort, I figured the fastest possible way to the ball was to run up the ramp and out the back opening. Good plan all the way up to where I had nothing under me and was flying for a second or two. But then I began to free fall. Fortunately, the ground broke my fall . . . unfortunately, the ground was really hard. It took a few minutes for me to get up off of the ground and sit out the next few rounds of fetch. Nothing broken or bruised—did anyone see that coming?

Humans do not understand why dogs fetch. They believe that it's all just playing . . . and it is fun, but there are more reasons than just playing. It's a lesson in loyalty, humility, and trust. We want to show our humans that if you give us a job, we'll do it until we're exhausted, and they can trust us to bring the ball back. It's an example, it's a lesson, and it's, well, exercise. We need the exercise badly, but we can get that in other ways. Chasing and fetching a ball is a simple example of going after something you believe in and returning it in trust. It's also an example of focus and humility, as we'll submit to pleasing our humans and run ourselves ragged to chase and bring the ball back. Humans are worth the effort.

Some dogs haven't perfected the game or are too stubborn and too proud to humble themselves to fetching, or they just don't care. There are plenty of humans who act the same way, and sometimes I blame their dogs for not teaching them. Humans need to understand that they should swallow their pride and fetch someone else's problems. They should never be too proud to help someone and even look like an idiot while performing some dead-end deed or chore.

Take running after a ball or a Frisbee with all your power, as fast as possible for as long as possible. Humans should, in the same way, put all their power into their job, marriage, and children. They should give everything they have to please and help others and humble themselves, even looking like an idiot to show others that they will tirelessly go the distance and that the others are worth the effort. Humans should run themselves ragged to earn people's trust; they should bring back the ball every time.

Can you imagine me throwing a ball and expecting a human to get it and bring it back? Imagine the stares and the looks you would get. Most humans don't have the servant attitude for fetching. They wouldn't simply drop everything and run after something to help someone else for no reason. That's what God desires, though. He wants everyone to have a servant's heart —to give when it's not asked for or expected.

He wants humans to serve instead of expecting to be served. Animals and humans alike are not here to be comfortable; we're all here to serve. God wants us to serve without having a second thought. Trouble is, humans think too much about themselves and how things affect them. God wants them to give joyfully and to serve without reserve. He wants them to fetch.

God embedded in me the desire to fetch. It's my favorite thing to do. I show my humans over and over my willingness to please them, to be loyal and humble, and the desire to earn their trust. Some humans have that embedded desire as well, but it can easily get clouded. Humans need to be reminded that they need to put themselves second, run after someone else's ball, and bring it back for them. Being humble and not too proud to fetch can make God smile.

Tom's Perspective: Dogs have a God-given tendency to be obedient. Humans have a tendency to be defiant. We don't like rules or someone telling us what to do. As the man of the house, I don't like being told that I have messed up or my way is wrong. Mango has taught me that being open to listening to others, especially my wife, is usually intelligent and certainly less confrontational.

God asked us to be obedient to Him. He has some rules, but those rules are to help us and certainly not hurt ourselves or others. Jesus, who is part of God, simply asks us to love God and love others the way we want to be loved. That's pretty simple, and it's the way Mango lives. It's possible that after learning from Mango, I might run after a stick. Okay, maybe not, but if she doesn't run after it, I'll go pick it up to keep from running over it with the lawn mower.

15

Did I Really Deserve That?

If you remember, we have a cat in the house . . . Kiwi.
Yes, they name the animals after food here. I just go
with it. Cats don't do much. Kiwi is smart but keeps to
herself a lot. She's good about catching a moth or a
bug that sneaks in the door when it's opened. Mostly,
she just lies around and eats. Some people say that
about dogs, but you and I know different. Kiwi sometimes (rarely) plays games with me, and they're not the
kinds of games I enjoy either. She will hide around a
corner or on the armrest of a chair, and when I walk
past, she will surprise me and paw at my face six or
seven times before I realize what's going on. It almost
scares the poop out of me. She paws at me fast . . .
those six or seven hits within about a second. Usually I
don't even know what hit me. When I realize she's
trying to play, I run after her, but she climbs to the
back of a chair or a place that I can't reach. I look at
her and say to myself, "I didn't deserve that."

Whether animal or human, we all fall short of what
God wants from us. Humans seem to believe a lot of times
that they deserve the food on their table, that they deserve a
dog lick, a raise, to be treated fairly, for no one to ever pull in

front of them in traffic, that the weather should always be sunny, that everything should always work out the way they want, and nothing bad should *ever* happen. But does anyone deserve anything? Bad things can and do happen, and God never promised that life would be comfortable. God promised that life would be challenging but that He would walk through it with us. The closer we walk with Jesus, the more challenging things can get . . . but they're challenges that make us stronger and better.

God is always trying to teach us things. We don't even deserve His teaching because we don't appreciate it, but He does it anyway. Things don't happen the way we want because we can't see tomorrow the way God does. We don't have a clue of what's going to happen, even in the next five minutes. We can only make choices on what we know and what has already happened.

God is somewhat like the author of a book. We are all the characters in this book. God knows the outcome of every choice we might make and what will happen because of it. He'll keep things from us in order to stop things from happening. He sometimes allows things to happen, good and bad, in order for us to learn. He knows how to make us grow stronger. He knows how to make us better, but not always in ways we would choose for ourselves. He doesn't necessarily care about our comfort; He cares about our devotion and love for Him. He wants us all to serve His purposes and work for the good of His kingdom, not our selfish pride, and not to make more money or get more dog food. He wants us to know Him and also make Him known to others. He wants us to be fulfilled and thrive . . . in Him.

God doesn't just say, "Watch this, I'm going to take this

job away from this guy and see how he does." God doesn't make bad things happen to us. Humans have free will, remember? Usually when something like that happens, it's from some human's choice. But, God promised that when we believe, He'll walk beside us and show us options to make the most out of the situation.

Think about it, what have you done for God? Why do you deserve any help from Him? You don't . . . He only does things for you because He loves you and wants great things for you. That's called grace. Grace is a gift that none of us deserve. Sure, we have all helped people. Some give time and money to their church, and those are great things, but are those things enough to earn the grace that Jesus gives us? Is that enough to earn the forgiveness for everything that we have done to hurt others, things that we know deep in our heart are wrong, things that go against what Jesus tried to teach us when He was here? Not even close.

He has given us the gift of grace, not because we deserve it, but because He loves us even after knowing everything about us. That makes my tail wag. Give your cares, your problems, your troubles, and your triumphs to God. It's all His anyway. He made it all. We don't deserve His grace and certainly don't deserve His forgiveness. He does it anyway, just for the price of loving Him back. And the more we love Him, the more He lets us know Him.

Dogs know this all very well. We don't always follow it, but we know He loves us and works miracles for us all the time. Don't think about how bad things are—think about how much worse things could be. Think about what great things happened today. God's blessings are amazing and always on time and perfect. Thank Him for it; He'll appreciate that.

Tom's Perspective: Mango has surely taught me that few things we receive are deserved. We give her a loving home, food, keep her clean, keep her up to date with shots and vet care . . . all not because she deserves it (although she's an awesome family member and she tries hard to please us), but because we love her and that's simply enough. Deserving it doesn't enter into the equation. God wants us to try hard at pleasing Him. He wants us to obey His commands and love Him wholeheartedly. But that's not why He gives us His grace; He does it purely out of love. We can't do too little or too much for Him. He loves us the same.

Break it down to the basics: God made humans and animals, but we couldn't live up to what He expected out of us . . . even the first humans. All through the Old Testament, people fell away from God, then came running back; they fell away then ran back. We sinned and sinned, and God said the penalty for sin is death . . . and it had to be some kind of living sacrifice. Then He sent part of Himself—Jesus, to live on earth to show us, face-to-face, what to do. Then He let Jesus be a sacrifice to pay the debt for all of our sins and shortcomings. In that, we can be forgiven for the prideful, idiotic, selfish, godless things we do by simply believing. We are free and clear. We don't deserve it at all. The more we do for Him, the more we see His wonders and get to know who He really is.

16

Speak to Us, Mango!

When Tom arrives home after his day at work, I meet him at the front door along with Cristian, who yells, "Daddy!" and gives him a big hug. Then it's my turn. It's the excitement of seeing him again, it's letting him know he's welcome, and most of all it means that it's time for him to feed me! I can't help but start barking and jumping on him to let all these emotions out. He certainly gives me a pat on the head and says, "Hi there, Mango." But pretty quickly, he tells me to stop barking because it's too loud. I have to speak to let him know that I'm excited. I want to tell him about the day we had here at home. I want to tell him how many rabbits and squirrels I scared away. I want to tell him I missed him and that I waited and now I'm hungry! All he gets is barks and jumps. How can I get him to understand?

Ruff and woof don't get me far on a driver's test, but they do get me a loving pat on the head, a small nibble, or a door open to go outside. Not being able to speak is hard. I can speak, and barks are complicated . . . but humans can't understand anything I bark. There is so much I need to say. Do you know how frustrating that is? I see so much, and I know how to fix stress and worry. I know that life with God is so good. But I can't say anything, I can only show it . . . kind of like playing charades but without using gestures. The problem, though, is that humans don't always listen to words.

Humans need to know about so many things that dogs know, but God didn't design the world that way. Humans have to learn most things on their own. If humans knew what dogs knew, so many things would be different. If they knew God was right here and loved them for who they really were, they would have more peace, forgiveness, and love for others. If people knew how much God did for them and how much Jesus sacrificed for them, they would have more compassion and trust. If people knew how many angels were within an arm's reach, they wouldn't look worried all the time.

If I could talk where people could understand, then where would I even start? God gave dogs an insight that most people don't have. I would begin by saying God is alive and God is real. Why do people even doubt that God is here? There is so much that God does and has done that should be enough to know He is real. Just look around. How could all this just happen? Flowers look and smell too beautiful, sunrises are too majestic, puppies and human babies are too amazing, and everything works too perfectly for there *not* to be a God.

Animals have the luxury of having spiritual communication with God. We know He is here and that His angels are constantly working for the good of everything here on earth. Humans have communication through the Holy Spirit, but the voice of God is much more subtle to them. Well, the trade-off is pretty big. Dogs get direct communication with God but don't have fingers or speech. People can pray out loud, but dogs can hear and smell twice as good as humans. Is that fair? It doesn't have to be. That's the way God made it.

If humans tried, they could understand our language. A bark is actually quite sophisticated. It's all about emotion. It has depth . . . it can be either a warning, a call out to other dogs, or a statement like I'm hungry! It can be, "Please let me out . . . please?" It can be "I love you" or "I want to play and distract you." It can be "I heard something and I need to check it out." It be can also be "There's an angel right here in the room."

A bark can mean so many things that only other dogs understand . . . but our tails are a different story. Our tails should be understandable for humans . . . that's something God designed to help humans see our emotions. Our tails are like our own language. Here's a way for you to decipher the language a little bit. When I'm happy, my tail goes around in circles. I'm a little weird, but it works. I have a beautiful tail, and it goes in circles when I want to play and am really glad to see someone. It goes up and down when I want to eat, need to go out, or am trying to say something important. It goes side to side when things are good and I'm content.

My tail, did I mention it's quite beautiful? It stands straight up when I'm alert and listening or I'm smelling something out of the ordinary. It is up or out pointing back but not all the way up when I'm proud. It is down when I know I did something a little bad. And it is totally tucked under, reaching for my stomach, when I'm ashamed or have found out that I'm to have a bath. Humans can know everything we're feeling . . . nothing to hide.

I can't say that for humans. They try to disguise most every emotion . . . especially sadness or fear. Dogs know people's every emotion . . . humans don't know it, but we do and that's how we can help. I can sometimes even hear what my humans are thinking, especially when they're angry or emotional.

Tom believes in God and has a deep passion for Him, but he still stresses and has high anxiety for things in his business. He worries about having to lay more people off, about paying his bills, shutting his doors, and going bankrupt. He doesn't understand that even if that happens, God will take care of them and things will be okay. His worry is showing that he doesn't trust what God has in store for him. I try to show him that things are okay and distract him or soothe him. He loves on me and rubs my back when I come up to him, but sometimes his heart isn't in it. He holds back because he's stressed and scared.

God is trying to show Tom that He is here . . . that He is quite active in Tom's life. The business will be almost completely out of money, and at the very last moment, God comes through with a project or some kind of money. It might be an insurance refund, an old invoice he forgot to send—something that is a total surprise but comes at exactly the right time. God has done this over and over, and finally Tom is beginning to see the miracles and the pattern. These miracles happen all the time, and Tom talks about them. He talks about how perfect the timing is. God is always helping and making things work out for his growth and learning and his best interest for the long run.

Still, he worries. I want him to just give in and let God do His thing. If Tom would simply give it all to God and realize that he can't control anything himself, that only God makes things work and happen . . . if Tom only realized that his worrying is a complete waste of time and it's robbing him of the time he could be enjoying his family and God's wonderful world, he'd be happier. I'm working on him, but ultimately God will show His glory.

Tom's Perspective: It would be so amazing to hear dogs talk in our language. But then in the same context, it would be awesome to hear the things that God tries to tell us. But think about it, would we listen after the amazement wore off? We hear people who are much wiser give us advice, and how often do we heed what they say? Think about it more . . . we can tell what dogs are saying if we pay attention and watch closely. They're clear about their feelings . . . totally transparent.

I have learned that from Mango. She can communicate well for not speaking my native tongue. The more I watch and try to understand her, the more I receive and benefit from her. The same goes with God. The more we give God the credit for things and try to understand why He might be doing something, the more great things we see Him doing. He gave each of us special talents, and He constantly speaks to us on how to use those talents to glorify Him and that gives us the greatest pleasure. The things He guides us toward may be out of our comfort zone, but when we step out of that comfort zone, He will equip us to do great things, rewarding things . . . things that are more rewarding than anything we can imagine until we do them. Listen. God is so good.

17

Loyalty Is a Human's Best Friend

I stand for my family. I'm loyal and I love them without condition. I was put to the test the other day at the park when we were walking on the main pathway. My family ran across another family who they seemed to know very well. That family had a dog with them as well . . . a little Chihuahua. I, of course, checked her out immediately in the usual way. She seemed fine, a little timid, but we were good with each other. All was fine until I noticed that my family was doting all over this dog. Friendly head rubs and coos are one thing, but they began to go nuts and love all over this little putz. I mean, I poop bigger than her. Normally I stand by and check out the surroundings to make sure we're safe and no bad guys or stray dogs can hurt us. This was getting out of control. They were holding this brown bag of droppings . . . kissing and nearly fighting over who got to hug her next. I had two choices: make a big distraction and stop this lovefest in its tracks, or be loyal and trust that I was still the star once we left. I decided my family needed my loyalty and patience more than embarrassment and trouble. I'm Mango and I'm loyal to my family.

Man's (and woman's) best friend. Every day, all the time. Have you noticed how loyal dogs are? Dogs are always there and always ready to please. It's what we do. It's what we're all about. We let just about everything slide off our backs. Humans can yell at us, they can move us out of the way, they can leave us outside all day, they can hit us or kick us, yet we faithfully run right back. We come back with our tails at full happy. Do you know why? It's one of our biggest jobs. God wants to show humans His amazing patience and tolerance through dogs. You can forget us; you can neglect us or act like we aren't even there. It doesn't bother us; we love you anyway.

God is the same way, but a billion times more. Humans can do anything and God doesn't leave. He knows humans aren't perfect and that you are impatient and fickle, but He loves you anyway. You can fuss, you can question Him, you can shake your fist at Him, you can believe that He is not big enough to handle your problems, yet He loves you. You can forget about Him and you can doubt Him or hate Him, but He loves you. Dogs are the best example of this. God assigned us to let humans know that He loves them completely and unconditionally, all the time.

Some say that dogs only have a seven-second memory. They say if someone doesn't scold us for doing something bad, then we don't remember why we're in trouble. That's not true. What is true is that if you yell at us or do something mean, it takes about seven seconds for us to forgive you. Well, then . . . we're an example of forgiveness as well. We forgive everything. We just want humans to love us. Nothing else. We will go to great lengths to show our love. And humans usually don't notice. We forget the bad things completely, and we don't ever let them come back up.

Now some dogs can be scared into submission and be frightened because of bad abuse or am extraordinary event like a fire or being outside in a bad storm. Dogs will not forget some of those things. That's not lack of forgiveness; that's simply being scared out of your mind and timid from then on.

We give and give . . . but humans have to give a little back. You have to feed us and give a little pat here and there. It's best to acknowledge we're here, just to keep a good relationship. And most of all, love us. The same goes with God—you have to give a little, but you get a lot. Actually, you get the world. If you believe in God and His Son, you have it all. You'll get the rest of time with God's power and wonders on your side.

Don't be misled, though. This doesn't mean life will be easy. That was never the promise. Believing in God simply means that He'll make it better, not necessarily easier. Like dogs, He is loyal and is always there. You can count on a dog. You know he'll be there for you. You know he'll care for you, and you know that no matter what you do, he'll always love you.

With dogs, there are few exceptions. With God, there are no exceptions. He'll always be there for you. He'll always love you no matter what, and He'll always care. He'll always provide wisdom and strength, right when you need it.

There is a difference. Dogs get distracted; God doesn't. Dogs are not perfect. We mess up sometimes, but God doesn't. Some dogs get angry, pouty, or selfish. I certainly have my days. God doesn't. Some dogs get jealous and do their business on the floor if their owners leave for too long. Cats get jealous and will do things in retaliation as well.

Some cats will ignore their litter box when they get angry. I heard of a cat who pooped in her owner's socks when she was reprimanded. I knew a dog that chewed up shoes when she was jealous. She would pulverize them to the point where they were not shoes anymore. She would get angry if her human would leave for more than a few hours. She would get jealous if the human had smells of other dogs. Her family went through many shoes.

In my house, I tear up napkins, but it's not really out of anger, it's out of trying to get food from them. There are usually ripped-up napkins either under the dining room table, on the front stairs, or on Tom and Michelle's bed. I don't believe they reuse them.

God is patient but jealous. He doesn't retaliate, but He does allow humans to choose their gods and sometimes allows that god to run their lives. He wants humans to learn. If He protected humans from everything, they would never learn. I look at the issues that Tom faces, and they're mostly the result of choices he made. The situation he's in financially is because he chose not to save money. Simple. It's not retaliation from God. God is loyal, all the time.

If I could be as loyal as God is, then I would be a much better dog. I pale in comparison and don't even deserve to live with this wonderful family. But God wants me here and has real work for me to do. Tom is such a worrywart. Why can't I show him that everything is going to be fine? As long as he has God in the front seat of his heart, he has no worries. If he would put God at the head of the leash and then let Him pull the leash and lead him, things would be so much more peaceful for him. God's future is always bright and glorious and never so scary that anyone needs to fret.

Humans can't see tomorrow; neither can dogs. God doesn't allow things to work that way because then we all would act differently. If we knew what was going to happen for sure, then we would prepare accordingly and avoid all possible troubles. We would never learn or become strong. It would be like having the test ahead of time and simply memorizing the test. What have you learned from that? Strength is usually gained as a result of some kind of struggle or issue we weren't prepared for.

Think about muscles . . . if they have no stress or resistance, no struggle or some kind of pushing or pulling against them, they will shrivel up and never grow. They have to be pushed, challenged, and thrown curves in order to develop and get bigger. The more they're used, the more they grow and become conditioned and stronger. If they're not used, they shrink and become useless. That's the way we living things are as well. If we aren't challenged and pushed, we never grow and develop. God knows that and wants us to learn and grow. That's why we're here.

I hear humans asking all the time, why am I even here? We are all here to learn. We are here to serve. God has plans for every living thing, but they won't be able to do those things until they're truly prepared. We don't come into this world ready for our jobs; we have to grow into them, and God will help us grow them. Even as a dog, I'm learning patience, loyalty, obedience, and love. God gave me the fundamentals, but every day I'm learning to be better at them in order to help my humans. When I become better at my jobs, I help my family more.

God will be giving me more tasks and jobs that I don't even know about yet. He'll prepare me for them if I let Him.

It's not that He can't prepare me . . . the problem usually is that I'm too stubborn to let Him teach me.

Humans are exactly the same way. They complain and get scared and upset when things happen that aren't in their plan. Sometimes they even get angry at God for the times when He is trying to help them learn and grow. The lessons are never easy, but if we look at the big picture and try to see what God is trying to do, we would learn faster and more quickly grow into the jobs we were created for. If we could face challenges with strong hearts, taking the punches with confidence that the ultimate outcome will be better than we could imagine, then we would stress a lot less.

God loves us all enough to teach us and guide us to the next level. We need to let Him love us. We need to allow the lesson to happen and try to figure out what the lesson is. Once we allow the possibility that God is trying to teach us instead of punish us, things change and the future looks much brighter and more fulfilling.

Tom's Perspective: Mango is as loyal as they come. We are fortunate to have and enjoy this dog and her steadfast loyalty. We have learned from Mango that loyalty is a trait God expects from us. After all He does for us, how could we be anything else but loyal to God? Sounds good on paper, but that's the problem. We aren't loyal. Not by a long shot. We make all kinds of things more important than God in our lives. He made us and provides for us in every way, and we give ourselves the credit. He gives us talent and we steal the praise.

We struggle to give God even an hour one day a

week. God, I believe, gets jealous when humans treat something else as their god. Money, careers, nice cars, nice homes, nice boats, or thousands of other things can be more important than God to people and become their gods. He'll go to great lengths to regain our attention away from these gods. Sometimes people don't understand when something out of the ordinary happens, something that adversely affects the things we covet the most. God might be trying to grab our attention back to Him. Instead, we get angry and say, "Why me?" Keeping our loyalty in check, using Mango as an example, can keep our lives much more content. Contentment equals smiles.

18

Can Dogs Tell Time?

The late summer, usually July and August in our country, are referred to as the dog days of summer. They're the hottest and presumably the slowest-moving days. I imagine people believe that dogs move slowly all the time and equate slow-moving days with dogs. I don't believe I'm slow and don't like the idea that a miserably hot day relates to a dog. Why don't we call them cat days? Better yet, why not call them "taco days" because tacos are spicy hot and people get slow and lazy after eating them. Just sayin'.

We dogs have a lot of time on our paws. Our time isn't necessarily wasted. We are on alert all the time. Even with our eyes closed we can hear something and be barking at a window at a moment's notice. Think about it . . . if there are seven dog years in a human year, then a dog spends a week (seven days) every day. So our time is important. We have time to think and time to learn. If a dog is impatient or gets bored easily, then bad things usually happen. Furniture gets chewed, underwear gets eaten, pencils get chewed, and toys get eaten. We wait . . . a lot. When our humans go to the store, to work, to church, or to school . . . we wait. We wait until they come home. They're our jobs, and we center what we do around what they do. That's what God asks us to do.

But we still need to spend our time carefully. Dogs are not so good at that. We worry about when our humans are coming home so much that we forget to do the things we should. We do usually sleep, which means we're rested when they come home, and that's a plus. Dogs are more reactors than planners. We usually only react to a situation and never spend time to plan what should be done.

With the jobs God gives us, we don't have to respect time as humans need to. We have to love, redirect, chase, lick, obey, bother, challenge, and more . . . none of which require time management. We understand the need for using time properly, though. Through God's wisdom, I have learned a few things about how people should treat time.

Take time. Take the time necessary to learn about people. (Think back to sniffing butts.) Figuring out people doesn't happen as quickly for humans as it does for dogs. Take time to understand what people are about and what you can do to help them. Also, take time to pray. God is there and wants to hear from you. He cares about what you have to say and what you want.

Make time. Make enough time for people to feel special. Make time for your family and for your dog. The rewards are heavenly. Be careful not to be a watch checker. Being on time to things is, of course, important, but don't be a slave to time. Relax on some of the things that give undue stress or pressure.

Give time. Your time is worth more than your money. You can give money and help some people, but when you give your time . . . you are giving of yourself. Nothing is more precious to others than your time and attention. Give time to help kids with their homework or projects. Give time to your parents; they get so wrapped up in things and they always need help. Give time to your neighbors. Find out what issues they may be having. Neighbors are the people who live near you, but also coworkers, clients, your church family . . . anyone you come in contact with. Everyone has issues. Many people don't advertise them, but people always have things going on and they need some kind of help . . . a shoulder, a paw, an ear.

Redeem time. It's hard to fix things that have been done incorrectly or wrong. To redeem is to try to patch things up. Take time to try to repair. Don't let time pass so that wrongdoings and bad treatment of others go unfixed. The longer things remain in a broken state, the harder they are to repair.

Cherish time. Time can never be taken more than once. It's one of the few things that cannot be reused. It's a one-time thing. Once it has been used, it's completely gone. Only memories, pictures, and video remain. Take care to relish today and not worry about tomorrow.

Honor time. Respect the time that you or others have invested. It's easy to get complacent after a lot of time has passed. When someone has given a lot of time to someone else, don't let time go by without a thank-you or a special something in return. My humans have invested a lot of time in me. They play with me and work with me, and I try to help and love as much as possible in return. It's not because I owe them. It's because I respect what they have done and want them to know that I appreciate all of it.

Waste time. Watch a five-year-old. That child couldn't care less about time except when it's bedtime. That child enjoys wasting time . . . he does it with a smile. Somehow as humans get older, they believe that if a minute is wasted by not cleaning, sorting, working, or planning, then the day is unsuccessful. Even when we go on vacation, my humans feel like they need to be doing things so their time isn't wasted. If humans would just stop worrying about wasting time, they would smile more.

Lose time. As fast as time goes by, try to do things that make time disappear. Play games, take a long walk, read a book, read the Bible, call an old friend, watch a movie, play with your dog. Life is better when you are not watching the clock.

Eating time. Okay, I threw that in just for fun.

Time is a powerful thing. We can't stop it or change it. Humans can only see where it has gone and how they spent it. They can do things because of it and make plans and do things during it . . . but it won't wait for them. They can use it to their advantage, and they can let it get the best of them.

Simply put, patience is trusting in God's timing. He made time in the first place. If you're waiting for something to happen and have no control over the outcome, then it's in God's hands. You have two choices—worry about it, which will not change anything, or allow the outcome to happen when it happens, and move on with your life.

Make sure that you do what today calls for. Find a chew toy and destroy it . . . that accomplishes two things. It helps get frustration out, and it occupies your stress so you don't spend valuable time worrying. God is already dealing with tomorrow. He'll be up all night anyway; let Him worry about it. He'll meet you there.

Tom's Perspective: On the surface, dogs seem slow . . . and some are. Mango will rest and sleep at odd times, but she's always at the ready. She doesn't sleep much at night, as she deems herself our security system. She will rest after everyone leaves for school and work, but will still be alert and listen closely for strange sounds and things that are out of the ordinary. Knowing that her time is limited, as all of ours is, she knows that things can't be put off until later.

Mango gives all of her time to us and is always available when someone needs a dog lying next to them. She's ready to hug when the time calls for it. She'll play whenever Cristian or whoever wants to toss a ball or toy. I have learned from Mango that there's nothing more precious that we can give someone than our time and attention.

19

Where Is That Lazy Dog?

Talk about lazy. I heard of a family who was more than lazy. One day when they were all lying down in their living room with their feet propped up on the sofas and chairs, one looked at the others and asked, "Is it raining outside?" Silence. One of them didn't move at all but said, "I don't know . . . why don't you call the dog in and see if she's wet?"

If you ask me, I have seen a lot more lazy humans than I have dogs. Sure, dogs seem lazy sometimes. We sleep when we can. A lot of times that sleep is during the day when humans are doing their human thing. But believe me, there are some lazy dogs out there. Barley, the hound mix across the street, is as lazy as they come.

Hounds seem to keep one eye open and the other two closed. Meaning most of the time, Barley is asleep. I'll lie down when things are slow, but I'm highly on alert. Outside in the backyard, the sandbox is a preferred place to lie down. It's cool and comfortable and in the middle of the yard so I can be anywhere lightning fast.

To me, lazy is defined as doing things the easiest way possible. Also, lazy is trying your hardest to get out of doing things altogether. With those definitions, dogs aren't as lazy as one might think. We'll finish a job completely and with great eagerness and won't try to get out of it, unless it involves a bath. Fetching, which is a job, is done with all-out running. Protecting . . . just show me a squirrel or foreign person anywhere close to my yard, and I can go from a full recline to a full chase in less than a neck scratch. Dig a hole after smelling a chipmunk or vole that might be underground and I won't stop until there's a good-sized hole and dirt is spread evenly. Dogs will do their jobs with passion and purpose. Lazy doesn't figure in to it.

Many humans, on the other paw, have a lazy tendency. I know a few who will work harder at getting out of work than the work would have been in the first place. Most everyone in my house, other than Michelle, will not finish a job completely. Washing dishes for most here means grabbing a dish and placing it in the dishwasher thing. They don't wash the pans on the stove or clean counters. Sometimes that's a good thing for me because I can jump up and lick the counter for stray food that wasn't wiped up.

After someone gets the job of cleaning the dishes, a learning opportunity almost always follows. This opportunity involves long speech talking about finishing the job and being proud of the job you've done. Most in this home will not pick up after themselves and even will leave their snack plates on the coffee table . . . which is a score for me.

Tom wouldn't necessarily be defined as lazy, but then again, he'll surely look for the faster, easier way of doing things. When he mows the yard, he'll use the riding mower. That's not an issue until he tries to get close to the trees, what humans call trimming. He needs to be using the smaller, pushing mower because he runs into the tree limbs and sometimes breaks them. Michelle shows him the limbs that he broke and tries to explain that he needs to quit using the big mower for the smaller areas. Tom agrees and wishes that he hadn't gotten caught.

When Tom gives me a bath, as much as I dislike it, he has to dry me afterward. As far as I'm concerned, I can simply shake the water off and run around the house, shake some more, and dry out on the furniture. For some reason Michelle doesn't like that. She likes me to be dry before I leave the give-Mango-a-bath room. Tom will dry me but not nearly enough. I still have water to shake off for a while. Michelle tells him that the dog isn't dry and he needs to do more. So I have to come back and dry more. At least I'm not back in the water.

Humans should take more pride in their jobs. God wants them to do work as if they were doing it all for Him. And in reality, they are. If a human doesn't do a job completely, then usually another human will have to go behind them and do it. When the girls leave unwashed dishes on the counter, those dishes don't somehow magically get cleaned and put away. One of the parents has to do it or make the girls come back and finish the job.

When a human is really stressed, their care factor sometimes goes down along with their pride and confidence. When you are stressed and worried about something, try to catch yourself and don't become lazy and complaisant. Keep your attitude strong when you are completing your jobs and doing them with pride. That will keep your self-worth higher and will keep your confidence in yourself much more positive.

Tom's Perspective: Mango, like my wife, sees right through me. They both know when I'm trying to do something the fast and easy way. When I'm worried, especially, I'll only do things halfway. I'm learning from Mango that if I keep my values higher during the tough times, I can improve my confidence, pride, and self-worth.

20

Are Dogs Selfish?

I only wish I were half the dog my owners think I am.

If you observe, if you really stop and look, you notice that God treats everyone like they're the only ones alive. That's the way He works. As selfish as people, and animals are as well, that's the way we want things to be. And, if you haven't noticed, humans act like they're the only ones alive as well. God doesn't necessarily like that . . . but He treats everyone like they are anyway.

God would rather we all act like we're the last ones that need anything. That basically means to be humble instead of selfish. What have any of us, animals and humans alike, done to deserve anything God does for us? God gives and we all take . . . how is that fair? When many pray, they simply give a Him a wish list. He does so much more for us than any of us know or recognize. For one thing, we have air to breathe, even though humans are trying to kill the air supply by removing more trees than the earth will replenish. And how many car wrecks did God help you avoid today?

Then there are all the things that God arranges for us to make life more fulfilling. He prepares where we dogs are going to live. Some dogs have the most wonderful homes and we can help our humans have love and experience great life lessons. Some dogs have the worst homes and have to work hard to help their humans. They get beaten or shoved outside and can't show love or teach their humans how to be patient, kind, or giving. Some dogs have no homes and have the dangerous jobs of teaching other animals about survival and safety. But God gives us dogs the tools we need to get our jobs done. He gives us instincts and wisdom.

Humans receive the same power. Humans get God-given tools to complete the jobs they were given long ago. Why do you think some humans are good at some things and terrible at others? Those are the God-given talents that humans are to use to help others. Some humans are great at teaching, some are good at fixing things, some are good at cooking, and some have more patience than others. It all works well together if the humans would not try to do things they aren't good at. I'm good at playing.

I see humans all the time trying to do tasks they can't do well. All they get is frustration. Tom is not all that great at building things. He and Michelle rebuilt their deck a few years ago. They did a pretty nice job and saved money, but it took a long time to finish, and while they were working on it, Michelle fell through the wood pieces before the flooring was complete. Her leg was a different color for a few weeks. Tom tries to help cook dinner sometimes. Dogs are hyper sensitive to smoke smells, but I'm getting used to the smell of burned pasta. That only happens when Tom is cooking.

Think about it, God is in the service industry. He serves us when, truthfully, we're the ones who are supposed to serve Him. He makes things work out so we can do what we were meant to do. God gives humans the talents to perform their jobs so they can buy food and have homes. God arranges for humans to meet certain people so He can get His plans completed, but this also offers joy and new friendships.

It's the same principle food servers use. They serve people food and take care of them while they're in a restaurant. If they're really good, the server will make the customers feel as if they're the only people in the restaurant. They develop a rapport with the customer and give them everything they need to have a pleasant experience. The server should go out of his or her way to make even bad situations—like the kitchen messing up an order or slow-arriving food—into better situations. If they're good, they can turn a bad situation into a better one just by their wit and charm.

God works much like that server. He treats us all like we're the only ones who need anything. We come to Him hungry and then we hope or expect something wonderful. We come to Him desiring satisfaction and amazement. He gives us total attention and gives us everything we possibly need.

But if nothing happens, we get scared and angry. If the server doesn't bring food within minutes of when it's expected, humans get impatient and upset. They complain and even want to get back at that server by giving a less than appropriate tip, if anything at all. They don't realize that this money is what the server lives on. It likely wasn't even the server's fault that the food was late. That happens with all of humans and God, doesn't it? If the answer God gives or His lesson of patience and waiting is not exactly what we want or expect, then we get angry and wonder if God is there at all.

Remember, not every day is payday. Not every day involves receiving a new chew toy or table scraps. Some days have great rewards and some days offer opportunities to give to others. If humans get a bad report from a doctor or get laid off from their jobs, they get scared and even angry at God for putting them in the situation. They have no faith that God is there with them and is working on the situation to make it come out better than anyone could expect. Even when bad things happen, God can turn them around to be something good. We here on earth have to blindly love God and trust that He will do what is necessary to teach us and improve us.

I heard Tom talking about a time when they were buying a house. They had their hearts set on a particular house. They signed a contract on it but could not sell their current home. Time passed and they found out that another buyer had bought their dream house. They were heartbroken . . . but they prayed and said, "Obviously, God, you have a different plan than we do . . . show us what you want us to do." Then, a few months later, their house sold and suddenly they had no house to purchase . . . and out of nowhere, unexpectedly they found the perfect house . . . the house they live in now.

According to them, it's ten times the house that they thought they loved and lost. It's in the same neighborhood, and when we take walks, we go right past it. Every time they say, "Wow, I'm so glad that we didn't buy that house!"

Can you see God at work here? Sure, they were disappointed because the house fell through, because they thought it was perfect. Then another, much better house was available a few months later, and Tom got a raise to be able to afford it. So, something much, much better happened. God is good!

Tom's Perspective: What Mango is showing us here is that it's *not* about us. Usually when someone is worried or upset about something, they're usually concerned with how the problem might affect them personally and little else. It's difficult to look at the bigger picture, but to eliminate chronic worrying and useless stress, we need to look outside our selfish lives and circumstances. It's not about us.

God wants our hearts. He's not obligated to fix our troubles (although a lot of times He will). He's there to fulfill our lives and teach us to love Him, figure out who He is, and show others who He is. If you are breathing, then God is not finished with you. There are many things to do for the sake of Christ, and we must be strong of heart and mind to do them. How do we become strong? Through adversity. We wouldn't choose the adversity, but it's the best teacher. God allows situations to occur in our lives to strengthen us. God takes time to be assured everything is right . . . everything! Consider what might need to happen in order for your situation to improve. Allow God to be God and make things right. Impatience doesn't fix things.

21

Look at Those Muddy Feet

When I go outside to do my business, play, or stand guard, my humans will sometimes wash my feet when I come back in if the ground is muddy or wet. My paws have a lot of fur around them so dirt and mud sticks and cakes on them. When I see a puddle of water or some mud, I run through it. Doing that is much more enjoyable and rewarding than running around it. Afterwards when I come to the door, I'm usually greeted with, "Oh Mango! What have you gotten into?" They look at me and explain in their best dog language that I'm not coming in the house with those feet. Trust me, they don't speak dog very well. I do understand the pointing and hand gestures, though. They aren't happy with me.

It took a long time for me to figure out what in the world they were doing when either Tom or Michelle would pick me up, one arm behind my front legs and one arm in front of my back legs. They would carry me upstairs and place me in the bathtub. "No, no! Not a bath . . . I'll never do it again!" I tried to bark to them slowly so they would understand.

On went the water and I would completely freeze.

Outside I looked brave, but inside I was frightened enough to jump over the top of them and run outside through the window. If they started getting all my fur wet, then it meant a bath and I was sunk. If they started spraying my feet only, then it was tolerable.

The water only hit my feet and they washed them with the shower thing. Thank the almighty Lord it wasn't a bath! What a relief. Somehow they could wash my feet without getting the rest of me wet. As they carried me up the stairs (Michelle is little, and my body was not necessarily designed to be carried by a small woman), I thought I was in trouble or, worse yet, that something bad was going to happen . . . like being locked in the bedroom. Sometimes they do that when visitors come. I don't know why . . . I'm the best greeter they have. I jump up and lick everything I can reach.

Once a visitor is inside, I try to get them to play with a chew toy. How giving is that? I don't offer a chew to just anybody, but when visitors come and I like them, they get special treatment. Of course butt sniffing always fits into the situation. I have to do a full background check. But Tom and Michelle believe I'm a little overwhelming to visitors, so they put me in the bedroom and close the door. It doesn't make me happy.

Once they finish washing my feet I can run out, free as a bird. But the first few times they grabbed me and carried me upstairs, I wasn't sure why they would be doing this. It was not normal or the way I thought things should happen. But slowly I began to trust that what they were doing wasn't going to be bad. They weren't going to hurt me. It was going to be okay. I trusted their intentions and their needs.

That's the way we should all trust God. He has only the

best intentions for us always. God will bend and shape us just like I would try to shape a chew toy. It may not be comfortable or even pleasant, but He has His reasons and wants to take us in directions we may not see. But trust Him; He does not make mistakes.

God may take you down a road that is confusing, scary, or unsure. But as time goes on, things begin not to look so scary. In fact, they usually work out better than you would ever imagine. Because as we go down this road that is designed to show us what we're made of, we see that we have strength, wisdom, or courage to face the situation. If we let God move through us and embrace the hardship or discomfort, God will not only strengthen us but lead us. God wants everybody and everything to trust Him, even through scary situations.

Some people believe that when something bad happens, God is punishing them. God doesn't punish . . . He helps us learn things. Many times, we reap what we sow (I heard Tom say this), meaning that we may have to suffer through issues that we alone created, usually against God's better judgment. God can remove bad situations, but many times humans still have to face the consequences they created. God wants people and animals to succeed and be content.

A few days ago, I got stuck between a sofa and a table. I couldn't get free and Michelle had to help me get out by moving the furniture out of the way. God wasn't punishing me . . . it was my choice that got me there. I was looking for a chew toy, and I thought it was under the sofa because I smelled something that seemed like it was the chew toy. I knew it was a tight squeeze but went in there anyway. God helped me understand that things were going to be okay, and He showed Michelle that I was in trouble. Michelle walked in at exactly the right time . . . before I panicked.

I remember Tom telling a story about a friend taking a child to the doctor. The child had an ear infection. It was painful and the child was afraid. The doctor had to inspect the child's ear to see what the problem was. The child had wax and whatever else in the way, so the doctor had to clear out the blockage.

Tom's friend had to hold the child down . . . screaming with pain and fright. The child didn't know she was being held down for her own good. She had to go through the pain in order to find any kind of relief. Tom's friend knew that holding the child wasn't pleasing or comfortable and that his holding her frightened her more, but he knew it was for her own good and that things wouldn't get better until this task was finished. His child had to go through some pain to progress toward improvement.

God knows the same things. He allows us to go through some pain in order to progress toward improvement. He sometimes has to hold us down in the middle of our misery to help us find our comfort and happiness. God sees the big picture and knows what's best for each and every being. He knows that sometimes we wouldn't choose to go down the path that will be best for us. The child wouldn't choose to sit quietly on the doctor's exam table and let the doctor dig into her sensitive and painful ear in order to make it better.

We're all like that child most of the time, even us dogs. We don't know what's best for us most of the time. God has to intrude into our lives and stir the pot to get us to move into the direction we need to go for our best interest. We usually can't find our true destiny until we grow through some pain. If humans and animals would try to understand that God is *always* working in their best interest, then they wouldn't be so frightened, angry, or impatient.

Even if our situation feels like we're being held down and put through misery, we can turn to God and understand that He is in control and will turn the situation into good if we let Him. Instead of complaining about our problems, we should explore them and look for ways to grow closer to God. God never promised a painless life, just a fulfilled life . . . full of growing and love . . . if we choose to allow those things to happen.

We're *not* put here to be comfortable. We're here to serve. Think about that . . . The Bible doesn't ever promise that you will be comfortable here on earth. We'll learn, we'll be shaped, we'll be asked to do things that aren't comfortable at all. We'll be put in situations to make us stronger and situations that will help us understand that God is in control and we're not. The more faith you gain, the more challenging things might become . . . but only to make you stronger. No one learns when they're comfortable.

God has ways of making Himself known, and if we simply open our eyes, He's there. God will arrange things so there's an answer for everything and a way out of the mess you are in. The key is . . . His timing. Trust in God's timing. You may not like where you are but take advantage of it. You won't be in this situation for long but use the time to thank God that He cares enough about you to help you learn and grow. Thank Him for wanting you to be shaped. He loves you even when it doesn't appear like He does.

Step back out of your selfishness long enough to realize that things are not happening against you, but they're working to help you. You'll likely be in the situation you're in until either you learn what you're supposed to learn or until you figure out that you're not in control of anything and God has your back.

Think of this possibility. God might be preparing you for something . . . something big. If you think of your situation as preparation, your perspective will change dramatically. God doesn't usually throw you into a situation without preparing you . . . or at least strengthening you through the process. We may pray for an uncomfortable situation to change, and God may say, "No, please be patient." He may be allowing a little time for our strength, character, and perseverance to grow. And like the child on the doctor's table, humans don't understand what's happening at that very moment, but if they allow God to shape and mold them, even if it's uncomfortable and a little scary . . . great things can happen.

He has big plans for everyone and everything. If we don't allow Him to shape us, some of those things will pass us by and He'll find others to take the role. It doesn't mean our life is finished and He's finished with us, it just means that we won't have the opportunity and the pleasure of being able to take that particular role in His plan. Doing a job for God is always rewarding. It may be uncomfortable and it may be different from what we planned, but it's always great and fulfilling.

Dogs are usually more willing to let God put us in roles and jobs; we know the satisfaction of doing His work. There are some dogs that turn their heads, and their lives are not as rewarding as they could be. It's sad to watch, but pride and stubbornness are not only human traits.

Tom's Perspective: Looking back on many of the difficult situations in my life, I'm beginning to see a pattern. For every difficult situation, I have had more than equal amounts of blessings resulting from them. Divorce, a miscarriage, getting fired, a major car accident, having the IRS file a federal tax lien on my business—all were frightening and stressful. I gained strength from each one of these things and, most importantly, I later had the opportunity to help someone else who was going through one of those exact situations. Each difficulty we face has a blessing, if not many blessings. Like Mango showed me many times, what might seem like a bad thing at first (muddy feet) is usually not as bad as we imagined it would be and usually turns out to be a blessing. I heard someone say, "I have faced many tragic and desperate events in my life; a few of them actually happened."

We humans tend to keep our biggest problem on the forefront of our mind. Everything else is a distant thought. When we face money troubles, usually those troubles never leave our mind—they're always there haunting us. All the while, there are countless amazing blessings all around us trying to get our attention. If we have our worry blinders on, we can't, or won't, see the wonderful miracles happening right next to us. Mango shows me over and over that I need to give my blessings at least equal time. The problems get some of my attention, but others in the house get my attention as well. Now about those muddy feet . . .

22

Stick Your Head Out the Window

It has only happened once. I hope no one else saw it. The whole family was in the car. They have told countless people about it. We were driving toward the park at the lake. It was a beautiful sunny day, a little on the hot side. And with my thick fur, hot can get uncomfortable really fast. I was in the front seat, sitting in Michelle's lap. She groans a lot when I sit there because I'm not necessarily a small dog. I always want to sit with my head out the window, and this seemed like the perfect time. So I shot up out of her lap and popped my head out the window. Bang, ouch, dizziness, laughter, embarrassment. The window wasn't opened and I smacked my head loudly and hard against the glass. Since then I always look up and check first.

Ever wonder why dogs stick their heads out the window of a car and seem like they're totally lost in the moment? You already know that dogs can smell things from a great distance. We want to catch all of the foreign smells. We want to take in all the wonder of these new smells and also see the beauty of God's creation. We dogs don't care what anyone thinks about us; we just let go and let it all hang out . . . so to speak. We want to take in God's glory and enjoy the moment. We know that God will take care of tomorrow, so we enjoy the now. We want to take time to let the wind rush through our hair and let our ears flap. Life is good . . . very good.

Why can't humans let go like this? It seems that the older humans get, the less they let go and let God show them beauty and pleasure. God is in control whether we like it or not. When we try to stop His plans or take the direction of a situation back toward our pleasure and comfort instead of God's glory, things usually go wrong. It's a pride thing.

Pride will take humans and dogs down a bad road faster than anything. Our goal should be to do things to glorify God, not ourselves. That's the secret to success. It's not about us. God will work in our favor if we do things for His glory instead of our own. It's that simple. People believe that God is complicated, and He is . . . but He's also really simple. If you do things for His glory instead of your own pride, things will work out, maybe in a totally different way than you imagined or perhaps even better than you imagined.

Ask yourself, am I doing this for myself or for the kingdom of God? My humans adopted Cristian. They did it because God asked them to. They felt God urging them; it was apparent. They brought him into their home and their lives. They did it for the glory of God, and it worked out better than they could have ever imagined. I know that Tom was worried about the whole adoption process because he thought he was too old. He knew that when Cristian was in his teen years, Tom would be in his sixties. He knew they would be caring for him for at least eighteen years.

Amid all these concerns, adopting Cristian has been one of the greatest blessings this family has experienced.

Adopting Cristian glorified God a hundred ways, but it also gave every family member new and wonderful blessings. They have a young boy who is simply thrilled with life itself, and every day is a new discovery for him.

Anything can be done for the glory of God. Christians need to always do their best at whatever they do, unselfishly and with a servant's heart . . . all to glorify the Creator. Eating healthy can be for the glory of God because humans need the strength and health to do work for Him. We should give our talents, our accomplishments, our job, our chores, our free time, our hobbies, our workouts, our careers . . . all to the glory of God. Then they become worthwhile.

Today is good . . . it always is. Bad things will happen . . . there will always be struggles. Great things will happen— sometimes small but still great. Every day has wins and losses, victories and struggles. We all would have no real purpose without having to deal with challenges. Motivation is born through struggles and challenges.

Give the day a chance, and it can be really good. Start out by praising God and thanking God. Thank God that you have another chance to do better than the day before. The day is downhill from there. Relax. God is in control. Today's struggles will end at some point, and new ones will present themselves. Today will also have its good side. But . . . we can grow from each challenge, *if* we let the struggles become op-portunities.

I heard a human say that no matter how big the storm is, it will run out of rain at some point. Everybody has struggles. I sense it in every human and animal I meet. They may not show it or say it, but it's always true. Everyone is worried about something, and sometimes it seems that God is quiet, but He is there. As Tom says, when a human takes a test at school, the teacher is always quiet. Same with God . . . He is the teacher and He wants us to learn, especially during tests. And God does test. He tests us so we'll grow. He tests us so we learn more about ourselves. He tests us to help us learn faith.

Just know that God wants you to learn, grow, and become stronger in faith and character. We would *never* choose to have struggles on our own, but when we have them—if we allow ourselves to learn and grow from the struggles and not simply complain and want them to be over—then we'll grow.

God has big plans for all of us. If we accept the path that He takes us on, learn, and allow Him to shape us, He can do with us what He wants, and it's always good. As with any parent (or dog owner), God loves us dearly and wants the best for us. He wants us to be totally fulfilled and always be open to learning and growing. That's why He allows struggles to happen.

The goal, at the end of the game, is to be as close to God as possible, understand what He wants out of us, and to serve Him to our fullest potential. He wants us to share Him with others. Make someone else's day. Having that direction simplifies our direction and makes everything else seem small. That is a dog's main purpose in life. Try it; you might just wag your tail.

On your last day on this earth, what will you be most proud of and try to take with you? It won't be money, fame, a promotion, or even a high-dollar car or house . . . it will be the love you shared with a spouse or a child or a friend or even a stranger. You would be most proud of opening someone's life up to the truth of Jesus so they could have the wonder of knowing grace and forgiveness . . . the joy of knowing that the One who created them loves them and that they're assured of ending up in the paradise of heaven. You would be most proud of helping make someone's day better. That is what life is about . . . not stressing about money or a car payment.

Times have never been more difficult, and the pace and pressure of this world has never been greater. I hear my humans talk about the easier days. I hear the old TV shows, saying things were easier years ago. But life has always been a challenge. We are not here to be comfortable, we're here to serve. Did you read that slowly . . . we're not here to be comfortable, we're here to serve. God has the only relief to life's dog piles. You are not defined by your messes, and He will help make beauty of your messes if you let Him. Lay your trust in His ways, His plan, and His glory, and you can find peace and calmness. The peace He offers is magical and transforming. Be content with where He has you.

No one understands God's way until they truly experience it. It's like the parent trying to explain the love of having a child to someone who has no children. It's like describing the joy of owning a dog to a person who has never had one. Maybe it's like describing the thrill of riding a roller coaster to someone who has never seen one. I haven't ridden a roller coaster because they don't allow dogs, but you see what I mean.

The thrill of having God in your heart has no match. It doesn't mean that troubles will end; it means those troubles have purpose, and the stress associated with them can be shared. God will meet you in the struggle and give you peace about it. Give God the challenge; He is much, much bigger than that or any problem. He can deal with it the best way for those who love Him. He created this place and those in it. He can surely deal with our little (and big) issues.

When the oldest daughter, Carolyn, comes home from college, I usually have to greet her with a jump that's designed to knock her over. I get really excited when she comes, but I can smell a lot of stress on her the instant she walks in. I have to jump and let her know that she doesn't have to take it all so seriously. She's worried about school and her grades, she's worried about money because she's paying for part of her school. She's worried about the future . . . life after school, dating . . . all that stuff.

When she comes home, she calms down pretty quickly, but I feel like I have to give her total dog love. You know, rub against her, lick wherever I can break through and find an opening. I jump up on her when I know I'm not supposed to, but she needs the distraction and she needs a dog's compassion. She isn't here all the time, so I have to give all to her in a large dose.

There's a lot going on in her head. She needs me to remind her of love, peace, and happiness—that God has all she needs. She tries to take it all on herself, much like her father. They're both worrywarts and stress magnets. Sometimes it seems they look for stress . . . like they try to worry about things . . . like they want to be in this state.

Maybe it's because they believe that if they don't stress and worry about the worst outcome, then the worst outcome may happen. Sometimes people will get relieved of a particularly bad situation but then say, "Sure, that's better, but it might get worse tomorrow." They can't seem to see that things will be okay. That doesn't show much trust in God. If we believe in Him and love Him, He'll make things happen that are always for our best interest. Things may not look like it, but later you begin to understand. Things are usually never as bad as they seem, and they always could be a lot worse.

Tom's Perspective: When I see Mango stick her head out the car window, I'm reminded to smile. We don't need to worry so much. Chronic worry is habit forming and life stealing. We easily can let it take over our lives and lose all sense of happiness and joy. Believe it or not, we have a choice. It can be difficult, but remember to see the joy around you, or better yet, create some joy around you.

Michelle made a great suggestion to me one day when I came home stressed and distant. She said to pick an item outside of the house, stop, look at it, and say, "The problems stop here and don't go inside the house." I picked a bench in the front yard near the door. When I arrive home from work, I get out of the car, walk to the front door, see that bench, and say, "My problems from work stop right here." God gives me strength to walk in and give my family a genuine hug and become a real member of the family. If I could, when I drive home from work, I would stick my head out the window, but I have a feeling I might get arrested or, worse yet, have an accident. I do open the window much more often now and smell the air like Mango.

23

What's That in Dog Years?

I see my humans sitting on the deck, talking, eating, reading books, relaxing. That's a good thing to relax and slow down. Tom's at work, of course, but all the others are here. All is quiet and calm. Time passes and they don't seem to care. Don't they know that I'm aging seven days to their one day? I'm getting a week older today. I grab a ball and drop it at Sophie's feet, not to distract her, but to get attention. Nothing. She drops it on the ground. "Come on! I need to play! I'm getting older by the second," I plead. I think I see a grey hair. Woooooof! I have aged seven hours in the last one hour. I need to make the most of it . . . I'm diving into her lap. Screams . . . that's a good start.

We dogs are here for only a short time. When we're able to look back on our lives, the time seems brief, and many of the things we worried about and had panic attacks about were really nothing to worry about at all.

Humans refer to a dog's shorter life as dog years only as a comparison to their lives. We dogs usually live anywhere from twelve to seventeen human years, and that's a long time if you think about it. Our jobs, of course, are to make humans' lives richer and help them through tough situations. We have a limited time to do it. If we had longer, we would probably not try as hard and just be lazy. God knows what He's doing and how to time things for our ultimate benefit. Humans have longer to figure things out and point their lives toward God, but even their time is short.

We're all here to learn and get along. We're to learn about God and what He wants us all to do, and we're to treat others as they would want us to treat them. God sent part of Himself, Jesus, out of paradise to try and bring us closer to Him and show us His love. Jesus showed us how to live and treat others, and then He allowed Himself to be killed as a payment for our sins.

In case you're wondering, we dogs sin too. Anything we do against the will or desire of God is a sin. The punishment for sin is death . . . it always has been. Jesus took the death and punishment that we deserve and put it on His own hands and feet. He took the beating and suffering that we should have gotten. Yes, we sometimes get beaten and suffer, but we don't do it willingly, and we don't want to take it when we did nothing wrong.

Jesus took it willingly and knew what it was for and He did nothing wrong. Jesus died, and then as only God can do, He brought Jesus back to life to show us there is more than we can see. He showed us that death is not the final stage. He showed that God is more powerful than even death and that He can do anything. There is more.

Anything is possible with God, and we can either be amazed by that or turn our heads and deny. I have heard that every day there is more proof that everything in the Bible is fact. I already know that, but doubters try to disprove it and then eventually find out that the places and people in the

Bible are real. Researchers are discovering that the stories in the Bible are supported by facts. Don't deny the truth of the Bible . . . it is really what it says it is. Most of it was written by eyewitnesses who risked dying for what they wrote.

God loves us like crazy. He goes to extravagant lengths to show us that. We can't wait too long to figure that out. If we do, we'll miss the best part of life. With the short time we have here, we're to make the best of our lives and allow God to love us. When we allow God to love us, we have to submit to His love . . . His correction . . . His plans . . . His timing. The interesting thing is we don't know how much time we have here. We may think we have a lifetime to finish what we want, but there is no promise of a long life. We don't know that tomorrow won't be our last day.

Dog years are short. Humans invented dog years so they can relate to how short our time is here on earth. We have only a few years to accomplish our plan. But all our years belong to God. We are here to please and serve Him, so maybe we should call them "God years." Humans usually have sixty to ninety years to figure it all out and carry out God's plan for them. We dogs have to get it right pretty fast . . . understand what God wants, do it the best we can, and be glad with what we did.

What if this was your last hour on earth? If you knew that, what would be different? You wouldn't have enough time to travel anywhere and check things off your bucket list. Would you make up with someone that you are angry or upset with? Would you quickly try to accomplish what you thought God wanted you to do? Would you just drop to your knees and say you're sorry for not trying to please God more? Most everyone would say, "If I had more time, I would play with my kids more; I would have spent more time with my parents; I would not worry about work so much; I would take time to play; I would have let my child eat that second cookie."

Dogs usually try to live as if this is our last hour. No regrets . . . simple . . . honest . . . true. Do what you know you are supposed to do. Love now . . . live now . . . play now . . . praise now. We already know we don't have much time, so we have to make the most out of the now. Learn from us. We have to spend time with our humans because tomorrow may not be what we think it will.

Tom's Perspective: Dogs have to cram seven years into one of our years. Talk about time management. I have learned from Mango that we need to live as if today is our last. No one knows if today is our last day except God. We need to try to live as a dog would. They don't look back to relive past mistakes; they don't worry beyond a few seconds even if they get in trouble. I have heard that dogs don't remember things after seven seconds. I don't believe that. I believe they don't care anymore after seven seconds. They move on to the next thing and live life to the fullest. I do need to figure how much Mango's food costs every month in dog money.

24

Wag the Dog

Dogs would make terrible poker players. Why? Because when they get a good hand of cards, they wag their tails.

As I have said, dogs are pretty transparent. Our tails are the secret to understanding our emotions. Our tails tell most everything about how we feel at that moment. Our tails don't lie. We can't make them wag when we're not happy to see someone. A human can say, "Oh, hi . . . how are 'yew'?" It's so great to see "yew" with that funny sound in their voices, when they don't mean it at all. They're saying in their minds, *Why didn't I walk on the other side of the street. How am I going to get out of a long conversation with her?I hope she doesn't really tell me how she's doing. I don't have the time.*

Our tails tell everything about our emotions. When my tail is between my legs, I'm ashamed or frightened. When it is up high, I'm on alert and have a mission. When it is wagging side to side, I'm happy and proud. My tail sticks straight back when I'm unsure or think I see something. My tail does one particular thing that many dogs' tails don't do . . . it goes around in circles like a propeller when I'm especially happy.

When my humans come home after being gone somewhere for a few hours or even days, I get so happy. I don't know when they're coming back; I don't know if they're coming back. I don't know if they're going away forever, or if they will forget about me . . . but when I see them, I'm totally overjoyed. That's when my tail goes in circles. It's a little strange, but that's just me . . . unusual but awesome.

Humans are certainly less transparent. They're hard to figure out. I wish they had tails. I can tell when they're happy, stressed, afraid, or sad, mostly by smell. But other humans don't usually even know when something is wrong; they're so wrapped up in their own world, they don't even notice the hurt all around them.

Most humans can't read other humans, and humans usually don't give out a lot of signals about their feelings. When they're ashamed, or if they're sad or scared, they try to hide it. When they're stressed or sometimes even if they're angry, they tend to keep it deep inside. Dogs don't have that luxury and usually don't care if others see those feelings. We just let it all hang out.

Of course, we don't care that we aren't wearing clothes, we aren't ashamed, and we don't worry about scratching or licking in places where humans would never scratch in public. I don't quite understand that, but I get it. Really . . . scratch where it itches; clean where it's dirty. Humans won't poop in public either. Other humans would give strange looks and get upset if they saw someone doing something like that. Dogs can get away with it. People believe we don't know better, but it really is more like . . . we don't care.

Dogs don't care what people think about us. It only matters what God thinks about us. I wish humans could get that. They would have a lot less stress. Dogs don't care what other dogs think about them except when there is an alpha involved. Then we have to worry about pecking order and who eats first, but we don't care about how we appear to them or any other dog. We do care about hygiene to a point. Baths and being brushed make us proud, awful as baths can be. Being the first to get patted on the head makes us proud.

Humans need to lighten up. Jesus says people need to have faith like a child to understand and find stronger meaning in life as well as to get closer to God. Most children don't worry about how they look. Why worry about what other humans think? It's likely they don't care much anyway. God wants all of us to stand up . . . not to blend in to be accepted. Jesus stood tall. He made a point and did not care if people talked badly about Him. When the time was right, He wanted people to take notice of what He was about. Jesus meant to cause a stir, to help people stop and wonder about God, His Father . . . and we should too.

The only way we can make sure people notice that we're on God's team is to be out of the norm. If people are quiet and always worry about what others think about them, then God's Word will never be heard by a lot of people. Jesus was quite out of the norm . . . that's how He made an impact and got people's attention.

The people knew something was different about Jesus. He spoke with authority. He did things that were radical. He loved and accepted those who weren't accepted or forgivable. He rattled the cages of the leaders. He stood out. He let His love and actions for God outweigh His worry about what people thought of Him.

Relax . . . God is in control. Relax . . . God loves you for who you are. If He can love me, a goofy, fun-loving, carefree dog, He can love anyone or anything. He knows everything about you, even the bad stuff . . . and He loves you just the same. Humans generally give a funny or disapproving look to anything unusual.

When you are doing things for the good of God's kingdom, take those looks as a sign that you're making a difference, not that you're doing things you should be embarrassed about. God is never ashamed of you . . . especially when you're doing things for Him. When you do things for Him, for the church, for the sake of others without expecting anything in return, then true joy is at your paw tips.

Tom's Perspective: What would life be like if humans had tails? Our lives would be totally different. We would know when someone is truly glad to see us, or if they were fake and wished they had never seen us. We would know if someone was about to rob us. We would know if a car salesman was being honest or not. I know, without a doubt, when Mango is happy to see me, which is all the time. I know when she's frightened. I know when she's expecting me to feed her.

I have learned from Mango to be honest with my feelings about others and myself. Being honest with myself has helped me see how crazy it is to have all this chronic worry. When I'm more transparent with my true feelings, I catch myself being withdrawn and distracted. I try harder to care and truly listen to others during a conversation. I try harder to smile more. If I had a tail, I would wag it more. Being honest and more transparent with my wife gives our relationship more meaning. Michelle sure likes it. I doubt I'll tell her I learned it from the dog, though.

25

Who Is Your Alpha?

Walking in the park with my family one day, we ran across some friends of the family. Their dog came up to me, sniffed, and quickly barked, "You are not an alpha. You are nothing and I'm in charge of you. Bow to me and understand *who* is in charge." I of course busted out in laughter and barked, "Get over yourself. I'm with the coolest family, much better than yours. I rule in my family."

Dogs can be leaders or followers. I'm more of a follower; it takes too much work and seriousness to be a leader. The alpha eats first, sniffs butts first, barks first, and is the first to growl and make mean faces to show who's boss. In dog language, the alpha will always say what the rules are. By reading minds, we know our place. The alpha can be taken down, but sometimes he's harder to live with afterward.

Dogs quickly get comfortable when things are spelled out to them by the alpha. When we get and understand the rules, most dogs will try hard to fit in and be comfortable. Some will cower when the alpha reprimands. I don't respond well to alphas that are not in my family or pack. Submission is okay and respect needs to be shown when it's earned. Alphas do protect their packs and will keep order when there are issues.

There are alphas in the neighborhood and they dictate many rules when they're out. When there is only one dog in a house, we allow the humans to be the alpha. We'll pick which human is the alpha and do our best to obey and follow. We submit to them.

I'm good with following humans except when it comes to following Jesus. I'll not follow the crowd then. If a house doesn't follow Jesus, then the dog will stand alone and try to display the love of Christ throughout the house.

Luckily, I have a Christ-loving home, but there are many times when I need to remind them of God's compassion and grace. Every day has new stresses, and even when my humans have trust, a new situation comes up and challenges their trust all over again. Trust isn't something that's beaten once and never needs to be dealt with again; it's a new battle every day. It does get easier as faith gets stronger, but that jerk, the devil, always tries to shake trust. God is stronger than anything, so the devil will never win, unless we let him.

In basic dog terms, an alpha is the dog or person we listen to more than others. They command and receive our respect unless we want to challenge it. An alpha does not need to be male. I have been in a home where all the dogs were female and there was still an alpha. That alpha may not even be the strongest dog; it might simply be the first dog of the house.

Other dogs that might be able to challenge the alpha don't, since they don't want to upset the pecking order. The alpha commands respect and will receive it or things are not right in the household. No one can touch the alpha's food, and the alpha will try to go through a doorway first. Jesus is my ultimate alpha, and I'll submit and respect Him for life and beyond. In my home, Tom feeds me most of the time, and we have a strong bond from playing and palling around. I love all the people in my house, but Tom is my human alpha.

Tom's Perspective: Dogs are pretty transparent when it comes to them showing who their alpha might be. Dogs will show respect (or fear) when the alpha is around, and they'll submit to that alpha, dog or human. We humans aren't quite the same. We'll choose our alphas, but we won't always proudly display or show who our alpha is. An alpha is the one we submit to and let overpower us. So many people or even things can be our alpha.

We can choose bad alphas. Money and careers can be our alphas. We can also submit to alcohol and drugs as well as to someone we're attracted to. I sometimes allow my business to be my alpha. I think about and submit to it before so many other things, like God, my family, my own life, and more. We humans need to put other things aside and allow God to be our alpha. Mango showed me how dogs can submit to alphas. She has allowed me to be her human alpha, and she'll submit and follow what I ask her to do. She'll choose. She doesn't allow other dogs, food, or even our family become too important. She doesn't allow God to be pushed aside and let things of lesser value, importance, and meaning become too overpowering. Whenever I allow God to be most important in my life, I don't have chronic worry. I don't focus or give unnecessary attention to the things that do not deserve it.

26

Go Fetch a Brick

I heard of a dog that would go nuts over a brick. The owners lived in a house that had a small pond in the backyard. This broken brick could be beside the pond, and the dog wouldn't pay any attention to it. But when this partial brick was dropped into the pond, the dog would jump in after it and not rest until it was out of the water. She would put her whole head under water and paw and bite this brick until she was completely out of breath. Then, she would come up for air and try again. This brick was nearly too big to put in her mouth, but she would somehow find a way to bite this brick and get it out of the water. And when the brick was thrown back in, the fun started all over again.

Some dogs are really smart . . . *like me*. Some dogs take their jobs very seriously . . . like me. Some dogs are unmotivated and don't take their jobs seriously. They care for their humans but don't follow through with their assignments.

And then there are dogs that are just plain dumber than a rock. Some like the one in the above story . . . because they don't know better. I don't believe the dog wanted to save the brick or had a major problem with it. The brick just didn't need to be in the water. I know dogs that chase their tails because it's there. I like to play, but chasing my tail isn't productive or even fun. First of all, I completely understand that it's *my* tail. It's not going anywhere. Two, I would get dizzy and run into a table. Three, humans laugh when dogs do that, and I prefer to be laughed *with*, not *at*.

Some dogs bark at the doorbell on the TV. *Paleeease.* Dumb animals still have a purpose. I don't have much use for them, but God does. They still have jobs to do and they try their hardest to pull them off. Dogs, even at the dumbest level, are loyal and devoted. They'll do what is necessary most of the time. They'll protect, teach, love, and show their humans the glory of God.

There are people who are dumber than dog bones too. There are some who, given the chance, would chase a parked mail truck. I don't see a purpose for them, but God does. God takes everyone's skill level and has a need for them. God has a purpose for everybody and everything. He has not made a mistake and given more brains to someone else. He has done things this way for a reason, and He doesn't need to tell any of us what that reason is. He loves all of us desperately—all the same—and all humans should be thankful for that . . . especially the dumb ones (I'm kidding).

Humans have become so impatient. They think it's all about them. If humans get caught in a traffic jam, they get mad and impatient. They don't understand that a few minutes earlier it could have been them in the wreck . . . they don't understand that they should immediately pray for those involved in the wreck and ask for God's healing and strength for them. Humans, while on the telephone, may get put on hold and get mad and impatient. It could be a great time to read the Bible or pray for a friend.

If humans don't get through a checkout line in the store fast enough, they get mad and impatient. It could have been a perfect time to meet someone who might need a smile to carry them through . . . to know someone out there cares. If they would only allow me in a grocery store, I would make everyone smile. That's just what I do.

Impatience shows ignorance. Anger shows a lack of insight and willingness to make the best of what is going on. Anger and impatience show that you can't control your emotions. God may be trying to bless you with something, and anger gets in the way. Humans and animals both let selfishness and lack of patience get in the way of God's glory. How many blessings have we all left on the floor because we didn't allow ourselves to see the blessings? It's downright dumb. Go fetch a brick!

Tom's Perspective: We all have our brick moments. We catch ourselves going all the way underwater to chase after something that has no more meaning than a brick. There are many things demanding our attention on this earth, but many of those things are just plain dumb. We can all get a little too excited about them—the all too familiar, "If I could only have *this*, then life would be better." Mango shows me every day that happiness is not found in things. Things, even dog toys, get old, forgotten, and chewed up. When we focus on loving others and giving undying devotion to Christ, we stop paying attention to silly, useless, unimportant earthly belongings. We don't get so impatient and begin to understand that even when we do stupid things, God loves us anyway.

27

We Are All Adopted

I remember it well. I was sitting in that cage for months. At first, I knew that the next family walking by was going to choose me. Then after weeks and weeks of disappointment and shame, I began to believe that I was not going to be picked. I started to feel hopeless. I was alone and afraid. Yes, I got food, but I needed what we all need—love and a home. When the lights were off and all I could hear was howling and barking, knowing that the chances were getting smaller that I would be taken home, I prayed. I cried. I listened. Then it happened . . . I felt it. God told me to be patient. Just wait, the right family hasn't seen you yet. "Be your best every day," He told me. I perked up and realized how crazy it was to feel so sorry for myself. God was working on it . . . He had it under control. I couldn't let the selfish, silly, hopeless feelings get to me. If I did, if I looked sad and depressed, no one would ever choose me, especially the family God wanted me to have.

A few dogs are born into their families, but most dogs are adopted. We are selected . . . picked . . . chosen. Some are rescued and some are purchased at pet stores . . . either is adopted in my vocabulary—limited as that may be. What an amazing feeling that is. I was in a lineup, basically. My humans picked me over all the other dogs. Naturally, I won . . . but it was more than a beautiful tail that got me the privilege, and my home. It was a tug from God.

I was the one for this family, this home. Being adopted is the most special feeling there is. I didn't do anything to deserve being adopted. They didn't know anything about me . . . they just chose me given limited information. They knew I was a jock, meaning that I'm very active and need exercise . . . a lot of exercise. The adoption center told them that. They came and visited me two or three times, played with me, along with other contenders, and chose me. I felt content. If I waited and persevered, I would have a home and a family that I could please forever. Woof, woof, bark, arrf . . .

Cristian, the five-year-old, was adopted from Guatemala when he was one year old. Out of the thousands of children available around the world, my family chose him when he was three months old. God, of course, helped them choose. Chloe was four years old when she saw his picture on the Internet. She said, "He's the one . . . that's my little brother right there."

God performed countless miracles to have the adoption materialize. I heard so many stories about it . . . adoptions were closing in Guatemala when my family started the process. They had forty-five days to do three months' worth of paperwork and other tasks, including getting a home study turned in. Everything got done faster than anyone thought possible. There was roadblock after roadblock, but each time the door was opened. Even congressmen and senators helped get through the government red tape to make sure this boy came home to live here. Those people were put in our family's lives simply to help.

Cristian did nothing to deserve being picked. He was only a baby at the time. He was chosen, and his life was changed forever. Now he's simply a member of this family. He's not treated any different than any other sibling. He's not anything but Cristian. He's wonderfully happy, and they say it seems like he's always been here. Adoption doesn't play into it now. That's just how he arrived here.

He's amazing. He's all boy—curious and intrigued by everything. He gets in as much trouble as anybody else and is loved by all. He and I have a connection. We play hard . . . during tug-of-war I pull him around the house. He takes a floor dive onto me when I'm lying down, and I love every minute. He hunts me down to play. Sometimes I hide to make things more challenging for him. I chase him around the house and then he chases me. I run up and lick him in the face. I don't have to jump up . . . he's the perfect height.

Then there's playing ball. He and I can play ball forever. It doesn't have to be a ball either; it can be a chew toy, a rag, or whatever. He throws, I retrieve . . . we both know our jobs. We were both chosen, and that feels great. I don't know what I did to deserve this family and this house. Actually, I didn't do anything. It was God's plan, and I'm good with it.

Humans don't always understand that they're chosen as well. When they give themselves up for adoption, so to speak, if they open their hearts and minds to allow themselves to be taken into God's family then they'll be adopted like me. Believe in Jesus, and you inherit the family. You don't have to do anything to deserve it. You have already been chosen. You just have to choose to accept. Christ has invited you into His family. Say yes. And once you are in, you're always in.

Why God does this, I'm not sure. There are some humans that I personally would exclude, but God doesn't. It doesn't matter what you've done, it doesn't matter who you are . . . if you simply give yourself to God and accept Jesus for who He is, you're in. If you give in and believe that Jesus is for real, that He, God's Son, lived here on earth, died, and then came back to life from the grave, then you're a part of God's family. Adopted . . . chosen . . . accepted and taken in.

I know that feeling and it's special. Only love can take someone like me in. You don't have to wait until you're not sinning. That will never happen anyway. You don't have to clean up your act. That will come because you will want to, and you will still make mistakes. Only love can take in someone who does nothing to deserve it. Only love could allow some of the lowlife humans I have seen in my life into the family of God . . . but He does. Only love would take a dog like me in. I'm not that pretty and I'm high maintenance. I steal food off the counter and I chew pencils anytime I can grab one. I chew up underwear when I find them on the floor, and I constantly want my back scratched. I don't listen to my humans often enough.

I turned and gave my life to Jesus. He already paid the price for mine and everyone else's hatred, selfishness, bad thoughts, lust (yes, dogs have that too), and everything else. God said in the Bible that the price of sin is death. Jesus willingly died to pay that price. Simply admit that you have done wrong, that you need forgiveness, and then try to not do those bad things anymore. Not a very steep price.

I still do bad things, but I know that I'm also not only

adopted into my human family, but I'm adopted into God's family. I try not to do those bad things. I try not to hurt anybody. Jesus knows my heart. He knows that I want to please Him. From there, it's all downhill. So I was chosen by more than one family. Man, I'm lucky.

Tom's Perspective: It would seem silly if a family, after looking at countless other dogs, carefully chose one, all the paperwork was complete . . . and then the dog decided that she didn't want to go, that the adoption center would be better than a dreamy, fun, exciting, fulfilling, demanding, hardworking, pleasurable life with the family. Who could imagine that? But we humans do it all the time. God has chosen us. *He* has picked us out for a life with Him. He picked *us*. But there are many who say, "Nope. Don't want that life. I don't want to be loved and have a life that involves God." Somehow, these people choose a hopeless, scary, depressing, meaningless life that's full of worry, defeat, and always searching for something better as opposed to a loving, meaningful, demanding, hopeful, pleasurable life that fulfills and is content.

Mango shows me every day that she knows she was picked and she's always grateful for that. She lives her life knowing that things could be a lot different, a lot worse. She was in a kill shelter, where they have to dispose of dogs that don't get adopted. Deep down, I believe she knew that fact and is completely devoted to our family because we saved her from that certain death. Jesus saves us from a guilty, desperate, hopeless life that ends in certain death and worse. If we so choose, we can allow ourselves to be adopted and then live our life grateful to the One who saved us.

28

Why Do I Steal Food?

I can't help it. I'm tall enough, so I can reach the food on the counter. The kids' table is even easier because it's shorter. There it is . . . my weakness. A piece of bread for a sandwich, a bowl of soup waiting for Chloe to come downstairs to eat, half of a banana waiting for Sophie because Cristian only wanted half. I can't help it—I have to eat it. Gone! Anybody see who ate that banana?

They feed me every night . . . I can't ever complain about food. They take care of me. It's just that I'm weak. Food is my weak spot. I know they get angry when I take food that's not for me. I know it's wrong; I know I'll get in trouble; I know it's a sin to steal. Sure, the Ten Commandments were meant for humans, but they apply to every breathing animal. I shouldn't steal or take things that are meant for someone else. God doesn't like it.

I try to stop; I try to turn away. It's the hunt, it's the curiosity of the taste and the rebel in me that makes me take a second look and go for it. It doesn't hurt anyone that I do it, but then again, it does. It hurts . . . me. I feel terrible afterward and I'm embarrassed.

You would think that since I have the special dog connection with God that I wouldn't steal food. You would think that I would try to be the example that God wants me to be. I want to be good for God. I know He cares about that greatly. I can't help myself. I need therapy, a dog whisperer. I need help.

I have been caught taking food right out of Cristian's hand. When he walks around with clementine slices in his hand, I wait for the right moment and snatch one away. He gets angry and tells Michelle or Tom. Then I get it . . . out to the backyard, alone. Was it worth it? Well, no . . . I'm not proud. You would think that my connection with God would lead me in the other direction. To look the other way and give instead of take. You would think I would not make mistakes or bad choices.

Some humans believe that when someone says they're Christian, they shouldn't make mistakes or bad choices. People are quick to point out a Christian's mistake or sin. They look at the believer as a hypocrite if they slip up. That's why many don't want to go to a church. For the most part, nothing could be further from the truth.

Of course, there are people who slip up in every walk of life, in a church or not. A Christian wants to please God because of the wonderful love that God offers. His beautiful grace makes a follower want to try harder to give instead of take, and not hurt anybody. There are exceptions . . . there are some really bad hypocrites . . . but Christians are as human as anyone else. Christians are not perfect, but they try to be. Christians believe they will be held accountable for their lives.

Everything and everybody struggles with sin. Believers try not to sin, but we're faulty. There are stumbling blocks.

Hopefully Christians will learn from mistakes . . . they will be truly sorry for the sin and try not to do it again. That's called repenting. But only the strength and grace of God can forgive us sinners and help us out of the crazy circle of sin we create for ourselves.

Tom struggles pretty badly with worry and stress. God says don't worry; don't fear. Having stress is basically like telling God that He isn't big enough to handle it. Fear is saying that God isn't big enough to handle your problem. Michelle tells Tom that the Bible says "Don't fear" 365 times, that fear is not of God. Tom knows God is real, but he lets the uncertainty of the future get the best of him. That's a sin . . . no, it's not murder or stealing food from a kid, but all sin is the same in God's eyes. It takes our eyes off God and puts them on ourselves. Anything that takes our focus off God is sin.

Tom needs to know that God is in control at all times and will take care of us in His way and His timing. We may not agree on what God knows is best, but where He takes us is always the best route, if we trust Him. Tom knows that, but he forgets it in the heat of a stressful situation. The possibility of not having enough money is, of course, scary and some-times he doesn't see his business being able to continue, but God sees a whole different view and knows what is best. He needs to know that making decisions out of worry can never be the right ones.

Tom needs to stop, take a breath, say a prayer, and trust God completely. He needs to see that in every situation, good or bad, in every outcome, God is spotlessly and totally trust-worthy. When we look back, we see where He has tried to take us, and it's always for our good. He wants us to learn things and to depend on Him and let go of fear and stress. God will take care of us.

Tom's business is going through a rough time. I have heard him say that income is less than half of what it was two years ago, that he had to lay off four people and he hated to do that. He felt responsible for those people and didn't want to lay them off. He didn't want to mess up their lives, but he had no choice. That had to be hard. Glad I'm not a human.

I also heard him say that he owes money to the IRS. I don't know who that is, but it doesn't sound good. I guess it would be like owing food to the alpha dog down the street. He is a big bully . . . more bark than bite, but I would rather not owe him anything. Tom is stressed about that and has lost weight from worrying so much. His face is much more frowny than smiley. If he had a tail, it would be down a lot. He doesn't play with me like he used to, and he doesn't play with the kids like he usually does. He stares a lot and doesn't talk as much.

I have got to somehow let him know that this worrying doesn't help anything. He has to learn to take care of the things that help today . . . and not worry about tomorrow. It doesn't help anything. God is in tomorrow already. He knows what's there and is working on solutions.

I hear Tom praying all the time. He prays more now than he ever has, and that's a good thing, but he's praying desperate prayers. God doesn't mind desperate prayers . . . He wants *any* kind of prayers. Tom needs to pray confident prayers and thank God for where things are right now. He needs to praise God for his situation and realize that God is trying to help him learn things. No matter how things turn out, God works for the best for all who love Him.

Tom loves God, so there's no huge problem. He *believes in God*, but he needs to *believe God*. God says that He will help. God is bigger than the IRS; He is bigger than the debts, bigger than the silence when the phone is supposed to ring with more business. He is bigger than any problem. I want Tom to know that it is all going to be okay. He and the whole family are healthy and they have a wonderful love in this house.

I'll continue to work on him and he'll be happy again. Michelle talks to him every day about having more faith and letting go of all these worries. She helps him a lot, but after somebody calls him about owing them money, he stresses all over again. He hates owing people money, but the business has been so bad he can't pay them yet. I know him; he'll when he can, but it's taking a toll on him.

God is trying to give him signs that it will all be okay. He sees those signs but still lets it all get to him. He knows he shouldn't stress about things, but he's still doing it. God knows his heart and is working hard on him. God has saved his business over and over, and Tom knows that. Doesn't he see a pattern? God has a plan and it will all be clear someday.

God knows that I shouldn't steal food, I know I shouldn't do it . . . He's giving me strength to overcome. I just need to stop and pray before I take the leap. I know I'll have food, so I'll try hard not to steal. I'll let you know how it turns out.

Tom's Perspective: Mango looks at me as if to say, "Why are you stressing? You're choosing to be a really bad worrier. Stop it! Smile and praise God. You have so much to be thankful for. You have all of us . . . and we love you. Everything will work out the way it needs to. God is good and that is all you need." I'm choosing to worry. Just like Mango chooses to steal food, I choose to worry so badly that I can't think of anything else. It has consumed me, and I feel hopeless and afraid. I have put my fear before my trust. I can choose to trust, I can choose to believe that God only has my best intentions in mind, that He's working on it, even though I created the problem.

If I trust Him, He'll make a way and I'll stand tall as His child. I can have peace if I choose to have peace. I can work as hard as possible on what happens today. I can stop worrying about what might happen tomorrow. I can only deal with today. Mango looks at me and seems to say, "You're getting it, Tom. Deal with today, and God will deal with tomorrow."

29

Do Dogs Really Pray?

Michelle is cleaning up the kitchen after the family dinner. She's pouring a pan full of pasta into a bowl to keep for another meal later. Many times at least one piece of pasta will miraculously miss the smaller bowl and land on the floor, which of course, is my territory. She pours and spoons out that yummy-looking pasta. I sit patiently. I have not been this still and focused for a long time . . . at least since lunch. I pray, "Please God, let one miss the bowl, please let *one* miss the bowl." God hears and grants when He deems it's the right thing to do. And this time it was the right thing to do because five pieces miss the bowl, and there is a dog who is smiling so big, she could eat a banana sideways.

Prayer is miraculous. Imagine . . . the One who created the universe allows us to talk to Him. He listens and cares, and He considers what we ask of Him. Prayer works, and God is listening. How He does it is beyond a dog's (or human's) understanding. It doesn't matter how . . . it matters that He does.

Dogs pray, by the way. We pray for our humans. Obviously, it's silent prayer. We also pray for food, but that's another story altogether. And for the record, God does understand barks. We see the stress and difficulties that our humans have and we ask God for help. We ask for healing and comfort. Most of all, we ask for forgiveness. No doggie's perfect . . . no human is perfect . . . we all need forgiveness. And God, through the sacrifice of Jesus, forgives all who believe and ask for it. That's nothing short of incredible.

If I were in charge (which would be ugly), and somebody blatantly did something that displeased me . . . I wouldn't be so tolerant. Imagine—you made the world and all the people and all the animals, and they did something to you that you considered unforgivable. Then they said they believed in you and were truly sorry and would try to never do it again. I would probably say absolutely no and wash them off my paws forever. But God forgives. All the time.

Used to be, the penalty for sin was certain death. People had to sacrifice food, an animal (yikes!), or something to try to pay for their sin. It was not easy. Then Jesus came along. God sent Him here to teach all of us how to live . . . to play nice with others and to love God. Then God allowed Jesus to be sacrificed, and that covers all sins . . . past, present, and future . . . for everyone who accepts this wonderful gift. That's unbelievable to me, but it's true.

So if you believe in God, love His Son, admit when you do wrong, and ask . . . you can be forgiven. That doesn't mean you can keep on doing it . . . you have to try your best to not sin anymore. Amazing.

My family prays. Of course, they pray before meals, thanking God for feeding them. I do too, but I do it afterward. Eating simply comes first; I don't want it to be taken away because they think I'm not hungry or something. The kids all pray before they go to bed, thanking God for the blessings of the day and also for certain things like the healing of somebody who is sick or something like that. That is all great and I have seen that in other homes I have lived in.

What is different about our house now is that Tom and Michelle pray together. They do it every day . . . out loud, and it's taught me a lot about God. At first I couldn't understand who they were talking to. Now I can see that this is powerful. It has power with God because I can sense a unique connection during their prayer, and it's also something I didn't expect. It bonds Tom and Michelle even tighter than they already were. When a husband and wife pray out loud together, they're at one with God. You can see the connection between the two of them and between them and God. It's like a triangle. Tom is on one corner at the bottom, Michelle is at the other bottom corner . . . and God is at the top. The closer Tom and Michelle grow together, the closer they come to God. Also, the closer they reach toward God, the closer they come together until all become one. It works.

Since they started this a few years ago, I have seen that their prayers have been heard and answered. I have seen that their marriage is even stronger than it was . . . and it was strong already. Recently, Tom has for the most part let go of his fears of the struggling business, and his trust and faith are stronger.

I have also seen that they read the Bible together or share devotions and talk about them together. If others could realize how this helps in every part of their lives, they would strive to do it. Woof, woof, bark . . . sorry, another rabbit. This is your last warning, you little pest!

Pray, out loud. When Tom takes me out at night before bedtime . . . he looks up at the sky and prays out loud. He talks frankly to God; he admits his failures and sins and asks for forgiveness. He thanks God for the wonders of the day and for the health and safety of his family. He thanks God for being God. He questions God, but he also says that he accepts God's plan and direction in his life.

I have heard him talk loudly to God and I have heard him cry out loud to Jesus. God certainly hears silent prayers and responds to them just the same, but when people pray out loud, it creates an intimacy that's deep. It becomes more of an honest conversation. A prayer that will change your life can be like this, "God please take away my [insert your struggle here], unless You need it to glorify You." That puts it all in perspective.

I believe people are more real when they pray out loud. Try it; God would love to *hear* from you . . . He would love to hear what's on your mind and heart. God knows your heart and already knows what you want . . . but He also wants to hear you ask for it. Think about parents—moms and dads aren't just going to give their child everything they know the child wants. Parents want a conversation and the intimacy of having their children communicate. Parents want to hear their children ask for things and talk it out with them.

God is the same way—He wants us to believe that He can take care of us and desires the intimacy of having us ask for what we want. He knows best and doesn't give us every-thing we ask for, but silent or out loud, God wants us to talk with Him.

Take time to pray. You have the unbelievable privilege of talking to the most powerful being in the universe. He will listen. He will also respond . . . maybe not in the fashion or timing that we would like, but He will respond.

Try praying together, out loud, with the ones you love . . . it's the biggest relationship builder there is. And dog, is it powerful!

Tom's Perspective: The power of prayer is transforming. Like any parent, God wants us to communicate with Him. He already knows what we need, but He still wants us to ask . . . to speak our desires and our worries. I have no special position or way to pray—sometimes with my eyes open or sometimes closed. When I'm in complete awe of what He has done for me, I find myself kneeling. My most valued time to pray is when I take Mango to our side yard at night before going to bed. I speak out loud and know full well that He hears me. I thank, I ask, I plead, I thank some more, I praise, I look for the best things that happened that day, and I praise Him for them.

The more thankful I pray, the less stressed and worried I become. When we thank God for His blessings for the day, we realize that things aren't as bad as our mind tells us they might be. It is liberating, though, to admit to God the idiotic mistakes I have made. When I'm praying outside at night, Mango seems so peaceful and, although she might be sniffing around at the time, I catch her listening and almost smiling.

30

What Goes into Your Ears Comes Out in Your Life

Tom and I are driving to pick up Chloe at one of her friend's houses. We aren't driving fast, but we aren't driving slowly either. I'm always looking around, not only from my open window but also toward the back and all sides. I need to know what's going on to try and protect my humans as best as possible. This day, a car is behind us. It has been there for a short time and is really close to us. The road has two lanes, but other cars and trucks are beside us. It's clear that this young man—yes, he's close enough for me to see his age—is in a big hurry and wants to drive past us. Tom obviously knows he's there but doesn't speed up, which makes me happy. After a few minutes, this crazy guy cuts between two cars in the other lane and makes his engine have a loud noise to blaze right by us. He has his window down and signals with his finger that he likes us. There was only one finger, so I'm thinking that he was trying to tell us, "You're number one!" I could hear, though, that the music he was playing (very loudly) was angry, screaming, and mean-spirited music on his car radio. Whenever I hear that kind of music, problems are sure to follow.

Dogs listen to music. No, it's not just noise to us. We hear it, but we especially notice its effects. We don't respond much to music, but humans certainly do. Music promotes and brings out certain emotions. If you want anger and hate in your home, then play or allow your kids to play music that contains hate and anger. If you want peace, hope, and more smiles in your home, if you want a friendly atmosphere and people to appreciate each other and get along more often, listen to Christian music. If you want encouragement and reminders of how much you are loved, play Christian music. Humans respond to music, even people who don't understand the mechanics of music. It speaks to their deepest emotions. Christian music has such passion. People who have gone through struggles and pain, who have found peace and understanding, who have lived and witnessed the transforming power of Jesus, have written and performed these songs. Even as a dog, I love to hear it. It's positive, uplifting, and reassuring.

My family has Christian music playing nearly all the time. They have it playing on the TV through the cable channel thing. They have it on in the car. I can tell that even when they're down, after hearing some uplifting music, their mood changes. The kids sometimes like popular music and play it, even change the station in the car sometimes, but they also listen to and play Christian music equally.

God speaks through music many times . . . I hear them say that God played a song just for them on the radio. He picked that song at the perfect time. Being the most powerful being in the universe, why not? Who says He didn't have that particular song played just for them . . . or a million people who felt the same way at that particular time? God does amazing things, and He's speaking to all of us constantly in the most surprising and unexpected ways. He's always trying to assure us that things are going to be okay. He doesn't want us to fear, worry, or have desperation. He wants us to focus on Him and not on our struggles and problems.

Try to keep the angry music to a minimum. I have been in homes where that kind of music is playing throughout, and everybody is tense or angry, there are few smiles and togetherness. Non-Christian music can take your emotions places that you don't need them to go. They suggest things that give you thoughts that make you stray from God. Even the news gets people tense and upset . . . keep it to a small amount and your home will be more peaceful.

Remember . . . it doesn't matter what you've done, it doesn't matter who you've hurt or lied to, it doesn't matter who you've disappointed or cheated. God loves you . . . desperately. He wants you to know Him and what He can do for you. You can find peace and have your life completely turned around simply by giving Him a chance. The second you turn to Jesus and acknowledge that He's more powerful than your issues, you instantly feel more peaceful. Everything changes. He'll always be beside you and will never leave you.

Dogs see it . . . it's all pretty simple, but humans seem to make it so hard. They let the possible disappointments of tomorrow mess up the blessings of today. Humans usually don't see all the beautiful blessings of God all around them. Just know that God is here and has the better plan. He doesn't make mistakes, ever. He doesn't 'steer people in the wrong direction or tempt them to do things they would regret. When something is out of your control, pray that God will take care of it . . . for His perfect will to happen . . . and then let it go. '

That's one of the hardest things to do, but it's the most freeing thing you can do. When humans try to control things they have no control over (mostly by worrying), they give God no credit for being God. Worry usually is a symptom that you don't trust God for doing the right thing. Most things never turn out as bad as humans worry they might be.

What about your eyes? Input through your eyes can last for the rest of your life. Some images you never forget. Scenes from a movie or Internet clip can play tricks on your mind. Dog years later, those images will pop up and take you to a bad place . . . an unholy place, a depressing place, or maybe a place of anger. Movies that have violence, heated moments, or words that my mother wouldn't bark . . . those images and scenes can work on your mind and heart in bad ways . . . and those effects may not be immediate.

Dogs have pretty pure minds . . . we certainly don't want to watch things that are precarious, but we can't exactly change the channel. If we bark or try to give humans a hint, they don't listen. "Not now," they always say. These things really do affect us all.

Why are people so angry when they drive? It could be because they watched a violent movie the night before, read a depressing book, or maybe they're listening to angry music while driving. Then somebody changes lanes and a driver has to slow down suddenly. They bark mean words and shake their fists and want to physically hurt the other driver or worse. Where does that get them? Now their whole mind is consumed with hate and revenge. There should be a law that you can't drive while angry.

Take care of what you watch and listen to, and it will impact how you treat people or act while you are alone. Many people say that movies are harmless, but they aren't. When you watch movies about things that are against what the Bible teaches, you invite evil things into your life. I have seen them, and they're much scarier than what's on the TV. Music can take your emotions either up or down . . . I choose up.

Tom's Perspective: Play Christian music all the time for one month and see what happens. I believe you will feel a change. That's all I listen to in the car and many times at home. Often the right song plays at the right time that helps me deal with the exact feeling or struggle I'm going through. Christian songwriters have such passion and such emotion that you can't help but be moved by their songs. A lot of the music they write comes straight out of the Bible. The music deals with many different issues that humans struggle with, and it gives a wonderful reminder that God is close by and will hold your hand through anything. Books and movies have the same effect. If you read a depressing book, your mood and attitude will be changed for the worse. You'll have to work hard just to get back in a good place after you're finished.

31

Right There, Behind My Ears

No one has talked to me or looked at me for hours. Do they know I'm here? I walk up to Michelle and give her the "I really love you" look. She then scratches behind my ears. I melt. I'm loved.

There is a secret place that will stop a dog in her tracks nearly every time. In my case there are two places, but not every dog has the second spot.

I always itch behind my ears. The problem is that my claws are too rough for that spot. I need a softer touch . . . no dog nails. The softer, loving touch of fingers and fingernails instead of sharp claws that dig a little too harshly . . . ahhhh. Scratch a dog behind the ears and you will have affection and loving eyes on command. You will have a dog melting in your hands. We basically freeze. When my humans do this, I know they love me. It shows they really want me around . . . that I'm appreciated.

Humans can make such a difference in someone's life with a loving touch . . . a smile . . . selfless affection. Dogs (and people) need touching . . . we're all wired that way. Without affection and touching, we feel much more alone. Hugs, an arm scratch, or back scratch will change the chemistry of a being. Instantly, when on the receiving end of the touch, you respond with peace, calmness, lower stress, and the feeling of being loved.

Show me a married couple who doesn't touch very often and I'll show you a divorce attorney about to make some money. It's so important! It's so necessary. It's one of the problems of living and being alone . . . there is no connection with other souls.

That's one of a dog's huge jobs. When a dog lives with someone who lives alone, we're helping to keep a connection of touching with our human. Even when people don't live alone, they can feel alone . . . because there is no touching, hugging, or scratching. Lying up against someone can make the difference. Scratching lightly can send a human into a different world for a few moments, which can change their whole outlook on the day.

God commands us to love each other; He wants us to help someone else feel important. Taking the time to caress our spouse, child, mother, or father (and yes, dog) is godly and can be the one thing that saves the emotional state of the most important people in our life.

I have seen people who have been alone for a long time, never feeling the touch of another. They can't hold hands or give a good-bye or hello hug. It's a foreign concept to them. Those things are so important . . . I wish I had hands, but our tongues are the closest thing to touching that we have. We can paw at people, but that has little closeness. When we lick a human or another dog, it is the affectionate touch that we're after. We can and do rub against our humans to create closeness and a special touch. And remember, we dogs need touching as bad as anybody or anything else.

Of course we use our dog tongues to clean as well, but

that's a different thing altogether. When we lick a human, it is a real expression of our love. We won't just lick anyone . . . it is a symbol of our total submission. It has to be someone that we accept as safe, loving, and completely trustworthy. When dogs lick someone, it is a sign that we would do anything for that person at that moment.

Let your love move outside of your body. The love on the inside of your being is waiting to get out and love somebody. Dogs freely show it and want to spread it. Humans need to learn to let go of their love. Your human hands are so incredibly miraculous. They're rugged enough to open a stubborn jar by squeezing very hard, and they're sensitive enough to feel a dog hair that floats onto their palm. Hands are strong and sensitive all at the same time . . . only God could design something like that. Dogs don't have that. Our paws are rugged enough to be able to walk on hot pavement or even in cold snow but are not nearly as sensitive as a human's hand. We can't share the intimate touch that humans can.

Take advantage of that touch . . . share the power of affection through a simple touch. You can't imagine the power that it has and the transforming effect it has on another. Reach out and touch someone (especially your dog).

By the way, the other spot where dogs (and even cats) like being scratched is right above our tail, on the top of our backs. It will stop us in our tracks. You have our total attention and you have our love. We know you love us when you do that. A simple touch goes a long, long way . . . we long for that.

Tom's Perspective: I know firsthand that when I'm troubled about something, a simple touch . . . a back scratch from my wife, a hug from a five-year-old . . . even older kids for that matter, will change so much. Mango rubbing beside me or giving a loving lick can change my mental state and stop a worry in its tracks. If you know someone who is worrying about something, even if you are carrying a bigger weight on your shoulders, give someone an arm scratch, a hug, a foot rub . . . and see how not only their mind gets a small vacation, but yours does as well. You don't even need to wait for someone to be worried; do it just because.

32

Watch Out for Poop on the Floor

I used to live in a home where the cat would revenge poop. When it was made angry, this cat would poop inside the person's sock that made it mad. So whenever it was time to get dressed, the human got a squishy, warm, smelly surprise. Don't upset a cat.

Outdoors, the world is my bathroom. After living with humans, I understand what a privilege this is. Pooping inside the house is bad. I try hard not to do it. I know it's wrong. That is for less sophisticated dogs. I learned that with my last owner. I got scolded and sometimes worse. I hold it as long as I can. When the family goes out for a long time, I hold it and hold it. I sleep, I cross my legs, I think about baseball; okay that doesn't work. I try very, *very* hard to never have an accident.

But there have been times, I hate to admit, that I have used this action as revenge. Not my proudest moments. Initially, revenge may make you feel good initially. Maybe I was mad about them being gone or not playing with me, but watching them having to clean up my mess made me feel bad. I knew that whatever I was mad or sad about didn't need revenge. I was not proud, and it didn't make me feel better at all. I felt worse. And I'm not good at cleaning after myself in these types of situations.

God does not agree with revenge. It never does what you want it to. Revenge means that we're judging and deciding on the punishment that others should receive. That is not our place or our right. God, since He created us, is the only rightful judge and wants us to leave the judging up to Him. He will deal with the consequences when the time is right . . . and only He knows when that is. God has the appropriate actions to help people learn. We need to leave the results to Him and remember to simply love instead of judge.

Woof, woof, grrrrrh . . . a chipmunk! Pardon me, I need to go take care of this.

Tom's Perspective: Mango is pretty good about holding it. She understands that cleanup isn't pleasant and doesn't want to add extra burdens on us. She also seems to understand that revenge only makes the revenger feel worse. It helps no one and is always short lived. Just think, we could cut road rage in half. "Mango, did you do this?"

33

What Is Love, Really?

Tom was staring at the wall. The wall was staring back. He was totally consumed. His confidence shattered, his self-worth was way down. He felt alone. I tried to show him my love for him. I licked his hand; I dropped my best chew toy on his foot. Nothing was making a stir. Michelle knew what was going on. She looked at him and said, "Look, I'm not going anywhere. I'm right here . . . right beside you . . . through anything and everything." He looked up at her and gave her a bear hug. That was all he needed. She loves him no matter what.

In my house, I see love in a lot of ways. And God stands at the paw of all of them. But one of the most defining displays of love comes from Michelle. She gives herself to everyone but herself. She does for all but asks everyone else for little.

Unless you have only been paying attention to your chew toy, by now you know that Tom has struggled deeply with his business. He's lost major projects and clients, which resulted in laying off employees, which then resulted in owing a lot of people and then being on the edge of bankruptcy, owing the IRS more than $65,000 in back payroll taxes. He worried day and night. It was chronic worry for sure. He lost his confidence, his self-respect, and his direction. He wasn't trusting where God was taking him, and was lost in despair and in a mild depression. I was worried about him.

Many spouses would have given up on him. Many wives would have lost hope in him. Some would have left him and broken up the family because of financial hardships. Not Michelle, not even for a moment . . . she remembered her commitment and held on tightly to God's promises. I could see it and hear it in her. She had enough trust for both of them. Tom had trust and faith, but the fear squashed it.

Fear is powerful if you let it take over. Fear and faith can't live in the same dog house. Michelle encouraged and always led Tom straight back to God. She would always say, "Give it up . . . give it all up to God! He is bigger than this business, He is bigger than any of our problems." And the clincher that always stopped Tom in his tracks was her saying, "Look, it's all just stuff, Tom. If we lose it all, we still have each other. I'll not leave you . . . God will provide and we'll be fine. I'm not going anywhere."

God was always close to them, and they were always fine. Tom worried for nothing. God somehow always made a way for them to eat and for me to eat. They sold things, they didn't go out much, they skimped . . . not on dog food, though. I always ate well. Amazing. They didn't do things that they wanted to do, but they didn't complain. Michelle would only buy clothes at the used clothes places. The kids understood.

Every time Tom looked sad or scared or upset, Michelle would stop him and remind him that things were not hopeless. They never are. They may look bad today, but hopelessness is only an illusion. People should never borrow tomorrow's worries for today's problems. You only need enough worries for today . . . God will handle tomorrow. Tomorrow's worries will look different when tomorrow gets here anyway.

God does understand when you doubt or worry; just don't let it consume your life. Doubting is human, and even getting angry at a situation and shaking your fist at God doesn't affect His love for you. He doesn't mind you letting out your emotions. He does mind, however, your indifference. Excluding God and not giving Him any thought or care is certainly troubling to Him. He wants your heart and your attention.

Michelle never wavered during this difficult time period. She stood by Tom's side every day . . . through his sadness, hopelessness, and even his anger and depression. She got upset with him. He listened. Tom yelled at God during his prayers. God listened. He prayed . . . a lot. He may have gotten upset and scared, but he always kept God in the picture. Michelle was there and loved him through it.

I heard Tom while he was standing out on the deck one really bad night, look up and ask God, "When will I be able to dance again?" I could hear God tell him . . . and it seemed like Tom heard it . . . "Right now! Dance *now*! It's the perfect time to dance. Today . . . right now!" I couldn't help myself. I jumped up, put my front paws on his chest, and attempted to dance with him. I believe he wished Michelle was there . . . but this was a situation that needed immediate action. I saw his outlook change within days after that. He was a pretty good partner for that little moment we had.

God wants us to dance even in times of difficulty . . . because there's always a reason to dance. The funny thing is that

Tom's life came together when everything was falling apart. He began trusting God before the business was saved. He felt close to God. He depended on God and nothing else. He was trusting God fully when things were still upside down and there looked like there was little hope. They were ready to go wherever God was taking them. Fear was nearly gone and they were ready to take it on together with God at the lead.

Michelle gave Tom the wonderful, unconditional love that we dogs try to display . . . she showed the undying love that people promise during their weddings. She showed that she really would be there for this family for as long as God allows her to be here. That's what a spouse is . . . a promise, a commitment, a vow to God and spouse. Some humans decide their marriage is over after little, insignificant problems. There is no future in that.

Tom and Michelle have been through problems in the past, and they will get through this one. Michelle showed true commitment during this difficult and trying time. That's as much or more than a dog could show a human. I'm proud to be here at this home. They're getting it. She played a big role in saving him from completely losing it.

Tom's Perspective: Knowing that my family, my wife, my dog, and my God all love me is transcending. Knowing that they love me when things are difficult, when I have no confidence, when I'm consumed with fear and doubt, when I don't love myself . . . is life changing. The way my wife showed me this powerful love changed the way I viewed love and marriage.

Like Mango taught me, remember to love. That's what Jesus told us to do: Love God, love others.

When we do that, we take attention off ourselves and allow the power of selfless love to truly free us. Mango loves without any expectation. She shows me that giving instead of taking fills the dog dish with contentment.

34

Watching People and Their Mirrors

People watching is my number one occupation.
Mirrors are pure entertainment. I love to watch humans when they happen upon a mirror. Watch them.
They brush a hand over their hair, suck in their
stomach, and stand up straighter. They fluff their hair
and pull their pants higher. We dogs use mirrors to
simply see how beautiful we are.

I imagine humans are nervous to see what other people
see. They want to be seen as more perfect than they are . . .
more perfect even than they see themselves.

I happen to love mirrors because I'm proud of my look.
My tail is gorgeous and I'm not ashamed to say it. If people
would be more proud of how they look and be confident in
who they are, then their stress would be a lot lower. Mirrors
don't lie, and people are more critical of themselves than
anyone else is. Humans worry because they sometimes judge
what others look like, but they don't want to be judged that
harshly by another.

The same thing happens with a camera. I was at a kid's
birthday party not long ago, and every time a camera came
out, people would either fix themselves up or run. When the
video camera was rolling, parents would act nicer to their

kids. They would smile more and would act more friendly to everyone around. Maybe they do this because they know it will be seen again. Perhaps they may have to watch themselves on this tape and want to look their best and be seen as a great person whether they are or not. See, dogs do notice things.

When we die, we'll be judged . . . animal or human. We'll account for everything we have done. No one has told me this, but I believe we all will relive any moment that affects another. I believe we'll live the moment in the other person's being. We'll feel what they felt, good or bad. We'll feel the hurt of the harsh tones, the growls, the snubs, and the judgmental looks. We'll also feel how someone else felt after we helped them through a bad time or after a reassuring, loving wet tongue lick. How rewarding would that be?

Hopefully, you'll have more of happy, loving playbacks rather than the mean or sad ones. If you knew you were going to relive every event, every word, like watching yourself on videotape, would you act differently? If you knew you would have to watch yourself again, would you try a little harder to have compassion, patience, and love? Remember that the camera is rolling right now. Check the mirror.

Tom's Perspective: What if that were true? What if we had not just a mirror to show a two-dimensional view of how we look but were going to relive how we treated others and see how they felt inside. That would change things . . . a lot. Mango doesn't have anything to worry about; her replay will be pleasurable for her to watch, other than when she tore up my pillow the other day.

35

When We Wait on Food

Did I mention that I like to eat? Whenever food is being prepared, I'm in the middle of it. It's kind of a given. No food is cooked, fixed, cut, thawed, shucked, washed, peeled, baked, broiled, toasted, boiled, baked, or blended without my presence. I hear activity in the kitchen. Tom sometimes tries to sneak food without my presence, but I hear him . . . always. Even when he cuts fruit, I hear it and bolt toward the kitchen. I'll not miss the possibility of eating.

You know by now that I have a good reason for listening so intently when things are happening in the kitchen. There's always the chance that something will be dropped. When it ends up on the floor, it's my territory. It's always a race to see if they grab it and rinse it off or I get to it first. Usually, I win and snarf it down, which is not the best thing for my waistline, but it's not a choice. I must grab things now, while they are in front of me. My humans do still use a vacuum cleaner, but they don't really need one. They have me.

One day, not long ago, Michelle was cooking dinner and little Cristian was hungry. He had already downed a smoothie that was left over from the morning, but he was still hungry, and he was not being patient. Every five minutes he asked Michelle when dinner was going to be ready. Most nights, he would ask her what she was making for dinner and then he would decide if he liked it enough to continue asking for it or not. Tonight, it didn't matter. He wanted to eat.

Every time he asked when his food would be ready, Michelle politely said, "In a little bit, baby . . . like I said twenty-one seconds ago." Every time, he would give a drab, "Oooooh." Nothing but this moment was good enough for him tonight. He was crabby and impatient. He wanted his food . . . now. He was hungry and I wanted him to have his food so he might drop something. He wasn't tall enough to be able to see what was cooking on the stove. If he could just hang on a few more minutes, one of his favorite meals, gluten-free pasta with non-dairy cheese and tomato sauce was going to be ready.

This scenario reminds me how we (humans and dogs) have little or no patience with God. We all want our answer or our resolution right now. We want God to answer our prayers pronto. We want God to fix the mess . . . usually one we created ourselves . . . *now*. We want God to make our promotion happen *now!* We want God to make the IRS go away *now!* We want that new job or project to happen *today!* We want the sickness to go away *this minute!* We want God to show His power *right now!* It doesn't matter that our answer, which is probably much better than anything we expected, is almost ready for us.

If we could focus on how wonderful God is and thank Him for what He has done for us so far, then we could be more patient for the answer to this current problem, whatever it is. God is always cooking up something wonderful for us if we only trust Him. He'll always have our best interest in mind when we keep His glory higher than our wishes.

Tom's Perspective: Like Cristian and his dinner, it is sometimes difficult for us to wait. Sometimes God wants us to simply wait and understand who He is and what He is about. If we stop long enough to understand what might be best for us and how God can perform the impossible, we can see His incredible wonders. He will not do His wonders until the timing is just right. He won't do anything until His glory will shine the brightest. Sometimes He won't do anything until all other avenues are closed and we know the only way the answer could happen is through God Himself.

His glory will shine if it's His interest that we hold most important. Be patient and wait for your answer. It might be the most wonderful thing . . . better than you could imagine. But remember, pasta with cheese sauce . . . and miracles . . . take time.

36

Are We Being Replanted?

Tom and Michelle have a big vegetable garden in the backyard. It has lots of tomatoes that grow along the fence. Many of those tomatoes, especially the little ones, grow through the fence and hang over in the yard, so I deem they belong to me. If they grow inside the fence, I can't reach them so I let the family have those. Outside the fence is fair game. Once I eat the tomatoes they have to go somewhere, and as we established early on, this backyard is where I go potty. I'm not sure how, but wherever I have pooped, in the next spring, tomatoes grow right there, in the middle of the yard or inside the arbor that's covered with a lot of leaves. Sometimes it might be where I chewed some of those little red yummies and they squirted out of my mouth before I could swallow. When these babies grow, then I don't even have go to the garden fence to eat a snack, I get to snack almost at will. I guess it gives a new meaning to "I reap what I sow."

I stay outside in the back when Michelle works in the yard. She does that a lot. I love being there with her. A few weeks ago, she walked up to a bunch of tomato plants that came out of the ground on their own . . . no one planted them. I have heard these kinds of plants being called volunteers, but she calls them God's plants because they just sprouted. Who knows how the seeds got put there.

She noticed that they weren't growing like they should because they were located next to the steps and between stones in the arbor. She knew they would survive but not thrive if left to grow in that area. They didn't have a lot of sun and were in the way of things in the arbor area. Michelle decided to uproot them and replant them in the vegetable garden. She pulled them up and put them into the wheelbarrow thing. She wheeled them over to the big garden to dig little holes for them. That's where I come in . . . that's my specialty. I'm a hole digger. I have the claws and the power. I could dig to the other side of the world if she would let me. She points and I dig. I'm not good at placing the dirt in one place; I'm working on that. I stop when she says stop.

While the plants are waiting to be planted, she says they're stressing. The leaves are starting to curl up. They don't like being moved. They're not happy. Once the dirt is ready, she plants them one by one. She gives me a pat on the head and says, "Good job, Mango." She goes inside and gets me a treat.

That night, she brings Tom out and shows him where she moved the tomatoes. He looks at them and sees that the plants are definitely not happy. He says they look wilted and sad. Michelle says just wait a little while and they'll be happier than ever. They need to get used to their new location and realize they'll get more sun, more water, and more room to grow. He says that hopefully they will get happy again . . . in a voice that doesn't sound so confident.

Sure enough, a few days later when Michelle took Tom

out to the garden to show him the tomato plants, they were happy, with pretty leaves and even little tiny tomatoes on them. Tom was a little surprised but glad to see that they not only liked their new home, but they were thriving.

I believe this is how God works in all of our lives. He knows we may survive and do okay in our present situation, but there may be a place where we'll thrive that may not necessarily be in our view. Maybe He might uproot us . . . and likely we won't like it. We might have to sit and wait for a little while before we get placed in a new situation. We may feel like we're wilting and falling apart during the process.

But when the situation is right, God replants us in a much better place. It might feel completely uncomfortable and wrong, but after a little time passes and we realize this is a much better situation, we begin to grow faster and stronger than we ever imagined. The gardener knows much more than the plant where the best place to grow might be.

The plant thought where it was growing was a good enough place. It would survive. But when moved to the right place at the right time, even though it didn't feel right and was even painful for a short time, the plant realized things worked out better than it had thought possible.

I'm not sure whether Tom is being replanted, but his life is surely being adjusted. Things in his life are being replanted—things like his priorities and his trust. Some of the things that were stressful for him might be in the process of being replanted so his life will be simpler. It looks to me as if God is not finished with his business because things continue to magically appear. Projects keep coming at the last possible minute, money comes unexpectedly when all hope seems lost. Only time will tell, but Tom needs to view all of this like God is making the best out of his situation.

I hope Tom will trust and stop worrying so much; then he can allow God to do His stuff. Whatever God does in Tom's life is right . . . He doesn't make mistakes. It might take some time and Tom might feel like his leaves are withering and the process is too hard, but God has it under control and will make it all work out in the long run.

Tom's Perspective: Life is a process of continual reinvention. If we don't allow growth, then we can block God's amazing and fulfilling plans for our lives. If you are in the middle of being replanted, remember that if God, the ultimate and most wonderful divine Gardener, is in the middle of your life, and you are leaning on His perfect wisdom and glory, you will have a better outcome than you ever imagined. Allow God to do His magic . . . even if it doesn't feel that great at the moment. You might wilt for a short time, but God will plant you where you will thrive.

37

A New Leash on Life

I can hear them getting the leash out of the little covered pot at the front door from anywhere in the
house. One time I heard it from outside in the backyard. The leash means I'm going somewhere. It means
they want me with them. It means a ride in the car, a
walk . . . something. It means freedom . . . almost.

For some reason, I get crazy excited when Tom or
Michelle gets the leash out. Why would I get so excited when
my humans put something completely confining around my
neck? Why would I jump around like a terrier over something they use as a control device?

I go nuts because when I see that leash, it means I'll be
going on a walk or ride with someone I love, usually the
whole family. I get to see and smell the creation that God put
right under our paws.

Okay, so at first, I am kind of crazy when I first go outside. I just want to run free for a minute. Humans don't understand that I need to run! When I have been cooped up
inside the house for a while, I need to run it out. I need exercise. When they play ball with me in the backyard, I can run
for hours . . . and that helps me from going nuts for a few
days. Even seeing the leash means good things.

So when we begin walking, I try to go all different directions and pull that leash out of their hands. I have done it before when we were camping in the house on wheels. We were away, so every time I went outside I was on a leash. That was okay with me. I loved smelling new smells and seeing new sights.

Then I saw a deer. That was it. Tom wasn't holding the leash tightly, and I ran before I even knew I was running. The leash snapped right out of his hand. The deer was unsuspecting, and I was going to catch that thing. Not sure what I was going to do when I caught it, but I could figure that out later.

I ran after the deer for a long while . . . man they're fast! I kept running and running. But soon it was gone. I was in the middle of nowhere in a place I had never been. If it weren't for my nose, I would be totally lost. I'm sure Tom and Michelle were scared because we were a long way from home. They probably were sure I wouldn't find my way back, and I wasn't completely sure myself. I heard them yell for me. I sniffed and looked hard for all the things I had seen while chasing the deer. To their surprise, I came running straight back to them . . . a bit dirtier than when they saw me last . . . but I found them easily. Sure, I could live in the wild, using my senses and street sense to get me through, but I have a job, and I don't have to hunt for food.

Needless to say, Tom loops the leash around his wrist now. One day I'll catch him slacking and make a run for it. I'll come right back, of course, but they need the exercise.

So here at home, after I get the leash on, I usually forget that it's on me at first and try to run. Wham . . . my body is running but my neck is not. That jolt is enough to make me give up running altogether. It's stronger than I thought it was. A leash drives me nuts at first. Then I get used to it and try to walk beside my humans.

I do pretty well until I see a squirrel. There we go all over again . . . I run before I realize I'm running. I take two powerful strides to help the squirrel become dinner . . . and wham again. The neck doesn't bend that way . . . stopped cold. That leash can be a pain.

I really don't mind it. I see that it's for my own good. I don't know the streets that well, and even though I'm sure I could find my way home . . . what if I didn't? Where would they be without me? The leash keeps me thinking about staying with my family, protecting them while we're walking out in the big unknown. A leash keeps me focused and helps me learn the right way to walk with them. If I stray off course, which is easy to do, they tug on the leash and pull me back in the right direction.

I probably could run hard enough and pull that leash out of their hands, but why? They take care of me. They love me. I'll accept the rules and the way they wish me to walk and act while I'm out here. The leash keeps me connected to them. We have an understanding and an appreciation for each other. But they rule, and I want to be under their rules and act the way they wish me to act. I show my love for them and that I want to be with them. I submit to them, although I don't always show it at first.

I rebel and try to get away . . . but after a few minutes of trying to do what I wish to do, I realize how great it is to be loved and have someone who wants the best for me. They know I could get myself in trouble. I could get lost, I could get hurt by another animal, I could go hungry . . . so many things I don't want to think about. I'm content with being under the leash. I would wear it inside the house if they thought that would be best.

If we submit to God and follow His loving ways, we have submitted to His control, but it's much different than a leash. God's control is nothing like that. Instead, we *allow* God's plan to take place. Even in a difficult situation, we don't cry and whine; we accept and look for the positive in the situation. We thank God for what situation we're in, we look for things to learn from the situation, and we work hard every day to improve not only the situation but our attitude toward it. Some people don't want to be under God's control. They want to go their own way. They don't understand that God's plan and manipulation is for our own good. He wants the best for us and knows how badly we can get ourselves in trouble.

Consider His control as more like we're walking alongside with God, holding His hands, rather than being on a leash. He really doesn't have a leash at all because we can all walk away from Him at any point . . . He gave us that choice. But to have true happiness and fulfillment, we need to submit to God for the simple reason that He is more (most) powerful and knows the result that's best for us. It's all in the submission.

He is in control and can handle all issues anyway. If we let go of our fears and anxieties and simply live for the challenges of this day, trusting God for who He is and what He does for us, realizing that God does not make mistakes, then we obtain peace and happiness. If we choose to walk alongside God and live by His Son Jesus' example, then we're content.

After I choose to walk beside my humans, then the leash isn't really even there anymore . . . it hangs down and has no pull on me. Only when I stray and lose my focus do they give a little yank and put me back on the path.

Don't get me wrong, God doesn't want to have us by the neck and keep us constrained . . . just the opposite. We are free to do whatever we want. He wants us to submit because we want to. He wants us to allow Him to run things and believe that His way is better than ours. He wants us to quit believing that we know best and don't need Him for strength, guidance, and life in general. He wants us to listen to His gentle tugs when we're straying off the path and doing things for our selfish pride. He wants us to give Him the kind of love that is giving and submitting. He gives us unconditional love and loves us desperately, but He wants us to walk beside Him.

Tom's Perspective: God has a plan . . . for every situation. Our charge is to live that plan. And we're supposed to LIVE it! Embrace your situation, no matter how difficult. When we learn to accept the things that we can't change ourselves and do our best to make the best of each situation, then we move toward feeling joy.

You are where God wants you to be. You will be strengthened by the challenges of this day if you allow it. Instead of feeling sorry for yourself, take charge and look for the best way to handle things. God does not make mistakes, and He is rooting for you. Sometimes God says no for an even greater yes. He doesn't want you to fail, ever. God is not punishing you. Move past the guilt of yesterday. You haven't reached the top, not by a long shot. The best is yet to come!

38

Wake Up, This Is a Good Day

I'm not giving up on Tom even though right now he is so distant. Even when he finds peace in the situation and seems okay, one little thing will take him right down that road again. He is impatient with all of us and quick to get angry. He can receive an email or call about owing money that will cast a look of worry and panic on him so fast that it scares me.

I have said that Tom has been stressing about his business and needs to believe that God has everything in control and all will be fine. This has been a three-year ordeal. Truth be known, he really lost it. He lost confidence in himself, in his God, and in his ability to be strong. Business was scary for sure, but he worried way too much over it all. God will open doors when it is time for them to open, and *no one* can close those doors. God will also close doors that no one else can open.

God wasn't finished with him in this place in his life. That was clear. Yes, God wanted things in Tom's life to be simplified, but the door was not closed. Every time a payment was nearly overdue, something would happen, and money to pay those bills or payments would be there in the nick of time. God was trying to show Tom that nothing and no one else was responsible for that money appearing but Him.

He lost nearly thirty pounds by stressing over the possibility of losing the business and being in a bad financial place. He worried about being able to feed all of us. He worried about laying people off because they were his friends; he worried about owing all that money to the IRS. They were in danger of losing the business, the office, their home, their possessions, their cars, and their ability to clothe their family. He was terrified to walk to the mailbox every day, wondering what bad news, IRS notice, past due notice, invoice, or bill would be waiting for him. He would constantly walk around the house, turn off lights, and grumble, "Turn off the lights when you leave a room! This stuff costs money!" Of course, the kids should do that anyway.

I can tell he doesn't even want to wake up in the morning. I sleep in the room with them, so I know. When he wakes up, it instantly hits him. He starts worrying and stressing. He doesn't know how it could possibly work out. I see the hopeless look in his face. He worries about money every minute of every day.

One day, he came home after having a flat tire. He took a turn too wide and hit a drain, which put a hole in the tire. It was on the side of the tire and couldn't be repaired. The other front tire wouldn't match the new one, so he had to buy two new tires, which cost $500. He said that he had the next two weeks' money planned out and they would barely make it as it was . . . how would he be able to pay for the new tires? He was freaking out. I know it was tough, but he needed to trust God.

That same week a project for $600 came through, and as

always, what he was worrying about turned out okay. Tom was at the time only paying himself about half of what he would normally make from the business.

He was always worried about things like this happening. Things that would cost money . . . money they didn't have. I heard that one day at church Tom was worried about not having money to give to the church. After talking it over with Michelle, they decided to give $50. A few moments later, one of Tom's parents, who was visiting the church that day, came up to Tom with a $50 check. His parents had eaten lunch at our home the week before during a family birthday party and decided to help pay for the food that was served, knowing that Tom was short on cash. That's just how God works.

But what's really unusual about that? God has provided for this family in so many ways . . . exactly at the right time. When there is a threat of being low or out of money, it seems like humans can think of nothing else. It never escaped Tom. He was consumed with it. Every waking moment, he was stressing about money. I heard Tom say that his business was operating at nearly a third of the income that it had two years ago. That couldn't be good.

And the worst thing, he was giving me cheaper dog food. I mean, not too long ago, I was getting raw meat, my absolute favorite . . . and now cheap, dry bag food. That hit way too close to home. Not only did it taste like beaver poop, but it made me want water *all* the time. When I drink water all the time, I have to pee *all* the time. When my family is gone for a while, things get really tight, if you know what I mean. It makes barking, uh . . . interesting.

Anyway, things seemed like they were going south. It was all scary to him, and you can understand that. The IRS put a tax lien on his business, whatever that is. It can't be good either because he was upset about it, saying that he couldn't get a bank loan to try and fix the problem because of the tax lien. He owed them a lot of money, like $65,000, with no foreseeable way to pay it and no business coming in. They could end up taking everything. He kept saying that it felt pretty hopeless.

Sure, it all sounds really scary, but fear is not of God. Fear of the future means that you don't have trust for the future. It seemed hopeless. I remember seeing Tom get food out for a meal and I could feel him thinking, "How are we going to be able to buy any more of this milk? We're spending too much on it. We are buying bread when we can't afford to pay for it. What can we do without, to make this stretch out? How will we be able to put gas in the cars next week? We need to stop driving somehow." He didn't want to skimp on food for the kids, but this was serious.

Something would always happen so they were able to pay for gas, for food, for clothes . . . for whatever they needed. It was taken care of right in the nick of time. Always. Every time. I don't see how Tom didn't see that. Well, he did see it, but he couldn't shake the fear of the next thing.

Once another issue came up about money, and there he went again, worrying about how to pay for it. He didn't need to. I know that God was taking care of them. Trust . . . it's that easy. Sure, they had to stop buying the extra things for a while and the whole family understood what was going on. Things can get a little dicey with owning a business. I heard that a lot. They didn't go out to eat, they didn't take any trips, they didn't do things with the family that would cost money, but they stayed together.

Michelle was always a rock for him. She stayed right by

his side through it all. She was an encourager, a person who pointed Tom back to God over and over, and a person who wouldn't give in to the tail-pulling hopelessness. She kept saying, "I'm not worrying; God is here." Every time Tom came home stressed, talking about a project being cancelled, receiving a bill that was overdue, or saying how he owed so much money to people and how in the world they would get paid, Michelle just said, "Give it up . . . Give it to God. God will provide . . . God will make a way." And He always did, without fail. I saw it; she saw it.

Tom tried to see it but was too overwhelmed and short-sighted. He walked around the house with his head down and no smile. He missed so much quality time with his wife, his kids, and with me because he was so consumed with worrying about money. It's time that he'll never get back. He had such a gift right in front of him . . . kids of every stage in human life . . . ready to play with him, sing to him, draw something awesome for him. And of course he had me, a bundle of happiness, a lot of fur and stress relief right in front of him.

He rubbed his face all the time . . . a clear sign of stress and worry. He scrunched his eyebrows, pressed his lips together, and was grumpy when I wanted to play. Whenever I would get in his way or drop a ball at his feet, he'd growl and walk away. Whenever I 'd lick his hand, he'd pull it away. I tried so hard to help him lighten up, but nothing worked. He kept feeling so hopeless.

Tom talked about owing money to small businesses that were having trouble as well and needed the money. He felt so guilty and ashamed. He told them to be patient and he 'd pay them when he could. He told God and he told Michelle that no matter what, these people would get paid. The family would have to eat, but these people would get paid somehow. But he didn't feel that God was going to help him do it.

Tom sometimes felt like God had given him all the miracles He was going to give . . . that He had used up his quota. He felt like maybe he had done something wrong, and God was mad at him. Tom had zero self-confidence . . . and felt like he was being punished and was going to lose everything and sink to the bottom. He felt like God was going to let him fall. I say, so what? Tom has us. We aren't going anywhere.

He forgot that he has God. God is right here, within patting distance. Exactly what else did he need? All that stuff he was worrying about was just stuff. It would work out if he let God step in and handle it. Tom tried too hard to make things work out himself, when God had everything already worked out. Tom wouldn't let go of the leash; he wouldn't give the reins to the most powerful force in the universe. He wouldn't allow anything to be a ray of hope.

He was full of pity and despair, and it almost seemed like Tom started getting so used to feeling rotten that he started to like and expect it. He couldn't see the little miracles that happened every minute. He couldn't see the blessings that made everything beautiful. He didn't see himself dancing ever again. He felt all of this . . . I could see it every day in his face and I could feel his feelings.

I wanted to paw him and bark, "Wake up! This is a *good* day! You're so blessed. We're all here with you . . . God, your family and kids, your beloved dog . . . we all will be here through whatever. Do you see? It doesn't matter. God will provide. Whatever happens, if it's in God's will, it'll be good."

How can a human climb out of something like that? How

can the most hopeless situation begin to give hope? How can a person feel like playing, like standing on his back feet and dancing in circles right in the middle of a big problem? For dogs, it's easy. We just look up to God and say, "Here I am, let me serve you however you need. Give me a lot or give me little . . . I'll say thank you."

Whenever a person or animal says that (and truly believes it), everything changes. God is the definition of hope. When our heart changes from, "Why is this happening to me" to "How can I serve you?" stress disappears. That's why we're here. Not just dogs. That's why we're *all* here . . . to serve God and others. We're not here for our own comfort . . . that comes later in another place. We're here to serve. And remember, we cannot serve God and have our own agenda. It all begins in our attitude of serving.

When serving becomes a true bone in your heart, then smiles are easy to come by, tails wag quickly, and dancing without music comes naturally. All humans look for hope . . . hope lives in Christ. It is rarely found anywhere else. The Spirit inside helps us find the hope that God offers, but we have to choose to see it.

God sent Jesus out of pure paradise and happiness down to this wretched place to show us all that hope is alive. Jesus showed us that through any issue or problem, we need to pray . . . then wait . . . and God will give us what is best for us.

Tom had a specific answer he wanted, and when God didn't give exactly what he thought he should receive, he panicked. Tom didn't allow for the fact that God knew what he personally needed and what was best for his ultimate growth and strength. God knows Tom better than he knows himself. Tom saw the short-term result of what was happening. God saw the end result and was trying to make the right things happen. Tom just got in the way. Humans get so impatient and don't understand the time needed for God to make things the way they *need* to be. Yes, God heard his prayers and wanted him to understand what he really was praying for and what he deep inside truly needed . . . and then He answered in His time.

Tom's Perspective: It's true, I made myself miserable. I was a chronic worrier. Mango was so perceptive, she saw it all. She tried so many things to lighten the mood and show her love and compassion. I could not get this situation out of my mind. I was stuck; I felt hopeless and that I had nowhere to turn. The answer was there the whole time. It wasn't the answer I was looking for . . . not even close. I was looking for a bailout. God was trying to capture my heart. I stopped waking up like my life was an accident and started living . . . for God. I have purpose and I'm loved for who I am.

39

Tom Is Fixed (No, Not Like That)

I haven't seen Tom like this in a long time. He smiles, he plays, he walks around confident and full of the Spirit. It took long enough, but am I happy to see him with so much peace! I'm ready to go outside and play with him, and the good thing is . . . he will.

It's not God's responsibility to get humans out of every little problem that they themselves created. Humans seem to think they don't need to live for God through the good times, but when times get bad, they blame God and get mad if He doesn't fix it for them. God's not a fix-it man. We are to serve Him. Most humans don't eat healthy foods, and then they get upset with God when they get struck with sickness, disease, and even cancer. They cry out to God, "Why are you doing this, why aren't you fixing this?"

All the while, they've been eating badly and doing things that truly destroy their bodies, so God's perfect design of the body falls apart inside. When things stop working the way they should, they get terribly ill and want God to magically step in and fix it. In His amazing plan, sometimes He will work miracles and fix the problem, but sometimes other things are needed and necessary.

Realize that God is not obligated to fix any problem we

have. He certainly will if it fits His divine plan. We don't need to understand those plans, we just need to understand that what He does is right. He doesn't make mistakes. He never says, "Oops." That's our job down here. God doesn't do things that are wrong for us in the long run. He always works for our ultimate good and, more importantly, He works for His ultimate good.

Many people go through money issues like Tom; many have tremendously more difficult times than his family is going through . . . but the difficulty is not the story here at all. The whole point here is *not* that God came to the rescue and bailed Tom out of trouble. The whole point is that Tom found peace, not resolve. He found peace and hope before God sent new business to him. Tom learned that through prayer, trust in God, perseverance, and a positive attitude he could find the true peace that God promises. He finally *believed* God.

I remember the night he got a call about a huge project that changed everything and basically saved his business. He was already completely at peace that night. Nothing had changed before that, they were facing large money issues, but Tom had figured out that what he had was more than enough. God (and Michelle) had helped him learn that whatever God had in store was going to be good. It might or might not involve having enough money . . . it might or might not involve being out of debt . . . it might or might not involve keeping his business open—those were just *things.*

Things will always come and go. The important puzzle piece is knowing that we're always in good hands and whatever is out of our control, we're to trust God with it and do what we need to do today. Stop worrying so much about tomorrow. Let it go and be patient with God's answer. God is not only working out things for your ultimate good but also for billions of other people at the same time. Things may just take a little time to work out.

I heard Tom say on more than one occasion, "God treats me like I'm the only one alive." Once he figured out how much God was blessing him, he saw more and more of the tiny (but wonderful) miracles that happened daily, hourly, even minute by minute.

God is doing the same for you right now. Look for the little miracles. Look for the things that work when they shouldn't. It's not a coincidence—it's God. God shows His face all the time, but his voice is usually not a shout, it's a whisper that can easily get missed, unless we're looking for it.

The one thing that kept Tom going was that he never stopped talking to God. Through the worst days, he talked to God. Sometimes he cried, sometimes he shouted, sometimes he pleaded, but he always talked. I heard him do it. I felt when he prayed in the car or at work. He prayed every night outside when he took me outside for the last time of the night. He prayed out loud. It was different for him to pray out loud. He knew that God was there listening, and it made a difference to be talking out loud and having a conversation.

I believe that humans should talk out loud to God. It makes a connection they desperately need. I knew that Tom always knew God was listening. He didn't understand what God was doing, but he didn't need to. When Tom learned patience and trust, everything changed, and he still has it now.

I have never seen him more at peace, even when trouble tries to strike. When something happens or has the threat of happening, Tom just says, "I can't wait to see how this turns out. I can't wait to see what God does." What a difference from, "Oh no, what now? This is hopeless." There were always angels around, and they're listening, helping, and blessing. God is in full control. Tom never had more problems or challenges than he could handle.

Dogs are serving beings. Serving others shows us that our own problems aren't so big and we really are blessed. When we help someone in need, our problems get pushed aside and we focus on another's need. Our minds then get cleansed a little, and we see our issues aren't so bad after all.

Dogs automatically serve others and understand that our needs are few. Humans can get their needs and wants all mixed up. What do humans really need anyway? Look at us dogs. What do we have to our name—no closet full of clothes, no paying job, no way to get any money, no house of our own, no car, no real possessions other than toys, no opposing thumbs, no hands, but we're completely content.

What's important to us? Pleasing God and pleasing people . . . and eating, of course. If humans could let go of worrying about all this stuff they think that they need, there would a lot more smiles around.

No human likes change, and I believe most every human's stress comes from worrying about change. Change can sometimes be the best thing that can happen. The changes in Tom's business have been the best thing that could happen. He doesn't have employees to worry about now, his expenses and debts are much lower, and he does the work they used to do . . . work he loves. He's happy. If he had a tail, it would be sore from wagging all the time.

Humans get way too comfortable with the ways things

are going in their lives. God certainly likes for things to change so humans can grow and not go through the motions without spiritual growth. He wants humans to experience His power and His ability to do amazing things. If everything was always comfortable, humans would never need to see God's power. They wouldn't even look for it or care.

If everything was easy and we had no challenges, humans would never amount to anything. Difficulties prove to be the best time for God to simply show His power and the best way for humans to see what they're made of. The best results happen from challenges and situations that are not comfortable.

Most humans don't know the strength they have. Tom didn't know his at all. He thought that he couldn't handle laying off his employees; he thought he wasn't strong enough to face IRS agents; he certainly didn't believe he had the strength to trust God to get him through the dark days. God showed Tom that he had strength, that he wouldn't give up during a crisis, and that he would be able to talk to others and tell them that God saved his life and his business.

God showed Tom exactly what he was made of. Tom needed to be shown that in order to know he had the strength through God to face tough things and that God is stronger than any human issue. He will give humans strength to be able to have hope.

Tom tells people all the time now that it was through the grace of God that the business is alive, and that happened after he was fixed. His debt is now under control and not hopeless any more. He doesn't owe any of the people that he owed so much money to. God provided the means to take care of the debt. Tom prayed hard to be able to pay those people, the people who were so patient and trusted that he was good for the money.

These were all people whose services he had used for a long time. They were all paid and Tom gave most of them extra for their trouble. The thing is, Tom's situation was never hopeless, just challenging. Nothing is impossible with God. Everything and everyone has hope. You just may have to search a little for it.

Even in the worst storm, God provides beautiful miracles, big and small, to prove that He's close by and never leaves us to face things alone. He will, however, use difficult issues to prove how great He is. The whole time Tom was facing these seemingly hopeless events in his life, God was displaying His power and glory. Tom just had to *choose* to see them.

Every week, Tom had some kind of bill or payment to make—utilities, bank loans, mortgage payments. But on *every* occasion, for the three years that his business was in trouble, those important payments were paid. The day before a payment was going to be thirty days late, when he was to get in deep issues with a bank, somewhere, somehow, he would get the money to pay it. Sure, there were late charges and many embarrassing calls, but they were paid. Every time.

Tom has realized that it all is going to be good, all the time, forever. He has no more chronic worry. Sure, there are times where he has stress, but it is never out of control. He worries a little and then prays, and then works hard to make the best of the situation. He plays with me a lot more and has gained back some weight. He smiles and plays with the kids a lot more.

I can see in his eyes now that Tom doesn't care where God takes him. Tom is happy to walk wherever God leads him and to face the challenge or help whoever needs help. He attempts to glorify God during work and at home. Sure, sometimes there are rough spots, but that's why we're here . . . to try and get it right . . . to learn. Remember, we're in school.

This is how Tom was when I first came to live here. His financial troubles aren't over, but he has found the trust in God that I wished he would find.

He has realized that the business is just a business. It doesn't define who he is. God defines him and gives him his direction. If God wants the business to stay open, it will! As long as God keeps the door open, Tom faces each day with enthusiasm and hope.

God, I believe, wanted Tom to understand that whatever happened with the business, with finances, with life at home, everything would be okay. He would still have all of us, and we would be taken care of. He had to make sure that his goals were pointed toward God and not pointed toward his finances. God has large arms to hold us tight in times of trouble.

During that trouble, Tom found how close God really is. He got to watch God from the front row. God wanted Tom to know that if he did things in the business that glorified God and not himself, if he gave praise to God whether things were good or bad, if he quit worrying about tomorrow and did what he had to do to make today great, then everything was much better and his stress was much less. Tom has figured out that he needs to count his blessings instead of his problems.

If you're living with regret, you're living in the past. And you're worrying about things you cannot change. If you're anxious, then you're living in the future . . . and you're worrying about things you don't even know about. If you have peace, then you're living for today and are allowing God to do His will in your life.

God blessed this family beyond belief. Out of nowhere, God provided a way for Tom to have enough money to pay off the IRS. He also gave Tom's business big enough projects to pay off the loans and leases that were causing so much hardship. Tom finally gets it. When the time is right, God will take care of even the worst issues and thorns. Tom learned that you have to be patient and try to learn what God is attempting to teach. Let Him work on things in your life that need improvement.

Faith is an ongoing lesson. Once you understand one step of it, God will take you down the next path. Be open to His lessons and allow Him to grow your strength. The devil will lie to you. He'll try to make you believe that God has left you alone, that He doesn't care, and that the impossible is impossible. If you listen hard enough, if you use your dog ears, you'll hear God. He is telling you that He's close and He'll show you His amazing power when the time is right.

Tom has such a wonderful peace about him now. It's so great to see him like this. Even when things get rocky, he doesn't freak out anymore. He deals with what he can and leaves the rest to God. God is the largest force anywhere; why not let Him deal with your problems?

Humans learn and grow through struggles. After a difficult struggle, humans find that things aren't always as bad as they seem. Tom says he's seen a lot of devastating things in his life . . . a few of them have come true.

Every person and every animal has adversity. We'll all have challenges and struggles that are designed to help us learn and get stronger. God gives us many opportunities to grow and be better. He puts obstacles in our way to help us find our destiny. We wouldn't choose those obstacles ourselves, but we can choose to learn from them instead of being angry and running from them. Then we grow, we learn, and we become the creatures God wishes us to be. If we choose to explore the challenges and let God shine through them, those challenges become glorious victories.

I'm proud of Tom and want to believe that I helped him, but truly it's his journey and I don't care who gets the credit. I'm most happy because he's found the peace that God desires for him. God's not finished with him in that business. When He is, the doors will close and others will open. For people who love God, that's the way it goes. He always does things that work for His good.

Tom is much happier. He trusts a lot more and he's walking alongside God. The whole family is, and that makes me proud.

My job is great and so rewarding. I'm blessed to be in it and live in this house. There's a lot of work left to be done, but this family has God. I can help keep them focused.

God loves them, like He loves you and wants you to know His Son—the One who came down out of paradise to live in a place where time confines us, where we don't know what's going to happen next, where things hurt, and where people are flawed, are not loyal, and don't do the right things a lot of the time.

Jesus came to this world to show us who God is. He was one hundred percent human and one hundred percent God. He knows firstpaw the pressures humans face. He can relate and understand you and your struggles. He lived to show us how to live; He loved to show us real love. Jesus told many stories so people could begin to understand God. Read them; things will start to make a lot more sense.

Don't forget who you are. You're the offspring of God. You're His ambassador. You represent Him to others. He is a part of you—like it or not—and loves you no matter what. He lives for you. Nothing is more important than God, nothing.

Live for Him. He will take you places you never dreamed could happen . . . and they will be good. When it is all over, there is nothing left but God. Woof . . .

Tom's Perspective: I wouldn't trade the difficulties and struggles during this process for anything. I learned more about God and got closer to Him more than any other time in my life. I got to watch God work firsthand. There were miracles everywhere. I was lucky enough to be able to watch them.

The journey through a difficult situation is price-less, but you have to be able to look it as a learning, growing, and strengthening process. Stop, look at your problems, and don't blame God, but rather try to figure out what He is trying to do. With patience and trust, you will grow much closer to God than by having things the easy way.

My family, including Mango, was the most pa-tient, understanding, and loving support I could ever have asked for during this time. I pray you are lucky enough to have a family like this. Go take on your problems head-on. Remember, God is already on them. Your life is *not* falling apart. God is piecing the solution perfectly together. Embrace it, enjoy it, be excited to see what happens next. Allow Him to be God. Don't simply believe in God; *believe* God. I pray He takes your struggles and turns them into blessings. He will bless you and you will see His blessing in action.

About the Author

Tom Baker has worked in entertainment, radio, and television for over 35 years and is owner of Cobblestone Entertainment, a television production company in Knoxville, TN. He graduated with a degree in Marketing from the University of Tennessee and is an executive producer, writer, producer, director of photography, video editor, and public speaker. He has worked on shows for A&E, Discovery, Oxygen, HGTV, Food Network, Travel Channel, DIY, and GAC, among others.

Tom has been a musician since age five, first playing piano and then switching to drums at age eight. Very active in his church, he plays drums in the contemporary worship band, teaches Sunday School to 8th and 9th graders, and produces videos for the worship services and website. Tom and his wife, Michelle, of 19 years and four children (Carolyn, Sophie, Chloe, and Cristian) love animals. They have four rescue dogs (including Mango), a rescue cat, and a fish. He and his family enjoy hiking in the Smoky Mountains, camping, and playing tag, card games, and board games past bedtime.

Contact Info
For speaking engagements contact Tom at: 865-250-0706
or email him at: tbaker4744@comcast.net

CPSIA information can be obtained
at www.ICGtesting.com
Printed in the USA
LVOW03s1047041217
558564LV00005B/91/P